Be the Flame

Sparking Positive Classroom Communities

Shane Saeed

ConnectEDD Publishing
Chicago, Illinois

This publication is available at discount pricing when purchased in quantity for educational purposes, promotions, or fundraisers. For inquiries and details, contact the publisher at
info@connecteddpublishing.com

Published by ConnectEDD Publishing LLC
Chicago, IL
www.connecteddpublishing.com

Cover Design: Kheila Dunkerly

Be the Fame/ Shane Saeed. —1st ed.
Paperback ISBN 978-1-7361996-4-0

Praise for *Be the Flame*

Be the Flame shares a message that is powerful, applicable, and vital for children and the education community. Shane Saeed breaks down how to make sure classrooms are a comfortable place for all students to grow. Her analogy of how a flame is made is creative, but leaves a lasting impact on the importance of details it takes for building a lasting and uplifting and positive classroom environment while fueling the flame in a sustainable way. This is the spark educators need and Shane provides the formula for turning that spark into a lasting flame!"

> —**Wade and Hope King,** Best Selling Authors: *The Wild Card: 7 Steps to an Educator's Creative Breakthrough*

Shane Saeed has written the ultimate guide to building relationships for teachers and school leaders. This book is filled with delightful anecdotes and brilliant strategies that are purposeful, clear, and beneficial for all the connections that grow within a school building.

> —**Juan Gonzalez Jr.,** Third Grade Teacher and Co-owner of Camp Learn and Grow

Be the Flame is a gem of a book that all teachers can benefit from, whether brand new or veteran. The author is a teacher herself, and her passion for her students and for education in general is evident on every page. She provides actionable steps for fostering values such as collaboration and class community (as well as community with co-workers and students' families). Through a "fire" theme inspired from her own childhood, Saeed charmingly motivates educators to be the light that draws others in."

> —**Shannon Olsen,** Second Grade Teacher and Author of *Our Class is a Family* & *A Letter from Your Teacher*

Education is all about relationships. But it's not just the teacher/student relationship. In *Be the Flame*, Shane does a great job of examining the dynamics of the classroom relationship, but also the relationships beyond the classroom with colleagues and even family. It takes everyone working together to create the best learning environment for students and this book, *Be the Flame*, creates a roadmap to that success.

— **Dr. Brad Johnson, Educational Speaker, author of** *Learning on Your Feet* **and** *Dear Teacher*, **Educational Speaker**

Building community is something all teachers should make a priority within their classroom settings, but it isn't always easy. *Be the Flame* ignited so much within me! Whether you are a veteran teacher or first-year, there are practical tips, strategies, and reminders embedded throughout this book. I love that *Be the Flame* is very easy to comprehend, offering several easy-to-implement applications that can literally be tried instantly. I found myself eager to get to the next chapter to learn more steps to building a classroom culture and community based on love, respect, and kindness. One of my favorite parts of this book is the "Be the Flame Actions." Reflecting on the thought-provoking questions will really help you become more aware and, ultimately, take the action that is needed. Shane has put her heart and experience into this book and that is evident through the words on each page. Her passion to build community and to help others create those positive environments will greatly impact students nationwide!

— **Megan Polk, Educator and host,** *The Literacy Dive* **podcast**

If there's one thing our world needs more of right now, it is a book like *Be the Flame* by Shane Saeed. I found myself invigorated and encouraged throughout but also able to walk away with many easily implementable ideas. Shane is a wealth of knowledge and writes in such an inviting way. I would highly recommend this to any educator who holds relationships at the center of what they do!

— **Todd Nesloney, Director of Culture & Strategic Leadership, TEPSA, author of** *When Kids Lead* **and** *Kids Deserve It*

Watching Shane teach for the last few years has been nothing short of inspirational. Now, *Be the Flame* allows *me* to capture her passion and relight my own flame for teaching. This book is more than another run-of-the-mill education book collecting dust on your shelf. It's an essential read, offering glimmers of brilliance that will undoubtedly make an immediate impact on your classroom. *Be the Flame* is the tool we all need to illuminate our teaching and transform our classroom communities!

— **Jessi Elder, Fourth Grade Teacher**

I love this book and it reads so familiar, as a teacher. I can see all the stories and anecdotes playing out in real time. It's like listening to a co-worker at the copy machine and so refreshing! Theory has met reality.

— **Derrick Carlson, Second Grade Teacher**

Be the Flame is an educational force to be reckoned with! From cover to cover and all in between, soon to be, current, and even former educators will love this book. The passion with which Shane tells her story creates a desire within the reader to redefine their craft and create lasting relationships within their classroom and community. Through heartfelt stories of teacher "flames" in her life, to practical action steps you can utilize in your own classroom, Shane delivers her message in a powerful way. This is not a typical required reading for teacher professional development. *Be the Flame* offers a practical, yet compelling way to cultivate positive interactions with students that will lead to the ultimate success.

—Kaitlin Johnstone, Kindergarten Teacher,
Co-Founder of Kind Cotton

As a veteran teacher, I can truly say that my flame has been reignited after reading Shane's brilliant book! Throughout the book, Shane provides so many personal and heartfelt examples of each topic, several of which are both pure tear-jerkers and flame sparkers at the same time. She goes above and beyond to give teachers action items that can be implemented into the classroom immediately after putting the book down. It's encouraging and obtainable! *Be the Flame* is a smoking hot must read for every teacher.

—April Graves, Fourth Grade Teacher

The highest compliment that I can give a book is that it's both impactful and immediately useful. *Be the Flame* does a fantastic job of meeting both of those criteria. Shane provides numerous practical strategies for fostering positive classroom culture and community, and it's very clear that she and her students have a lot of fun together. This book is a worthy addition to educators' bookshelves. Be sure to follow Shane on social media, too, since she shares a variety of pragmatic tips and resources every week!

—Dr. Scott McLeod, Associate Professor, University of Colorado Denver, and Founding Director, CASTLE

Shane's enthusiasm and passion for creating positive classroom communities is infectious! Shane does an excellent job of sharing her own classroom experiences and giving easy-to- implement ideas for teachers to try in their classrooms right away. I love the way she explains, in detail, how she models and practices with collaborative groups in the classroom. Personally, I cannot wait to implement all the class bonding activities that I learned from Shane to help build trust and respect among students. *Be the Flame* is a must read for all educators!

—Katie Gillespie, Third Grade Teacher

Be the Flame is truly an inspiring read. This book gives even veteran teachers fresh ideas for making vital connections with students. After 15 years of teaching, I've never read a book that has stirred my enthusiasm like *Be the Flame*. All educators, from newcomers to those with vast experience, should have this on their must-read list.

—Amy McKinney, Third Grade Teacher

Teachers must walk through fires and put them out constantly on a daily basis. They also rise from the ashes after life-changing experiences each year in their class. As a classroom teacher, I'm always looking to unlearn and learn and *Be the Flame* is a beautiful example of reflection and lessons that are applicable right away. Shane beautifully embodies the experiences we run into and how to overcome and brighten our classroom endeavors. Building a community of learners is no small undertaking, but *Be the Flame* makes it seem achievable.

—Anisa Khandwalla, Middle School Math Teacher

Shane has beautifully captured why the "spark" is so important in teaching and must be continuously lit. This book is not just for one type of educator, it's for all educators —veterans, newbies, those wanting to be in education. This is a book that should be read by all before the start of their teaching year. Lots of great ideas and very important reminders. It's like the idea of keeping the engine strong for the train to keep running. As educators, we need to keep that fire going to keep those relationships with our students, parents, and colleagues positive, respectful, and fresh.

—Krystin Simmons-Reese, Third Grade Teacher

Shane Saeed guides teachers to build an effective and supportive classroom community with easy-to-implement ideas. This book is the kind of book I wish I had at the start of my teaching career, and I can't wait to implement it now. If you're looking to foster a supportive and collaborative classroom community-read this book!

—Keanna Funderburk, Fifth Grade Teacher

Whether you consider yourself a new or experienced teacher, Shane Saeed writes to the curious, ever-learning, and ever-changing soul of all educators. *Be the Flame* not only prompts you to intentionally reflect on your teaching practices, but also provides a plethora of tangible tips, games, and activities you can take straight to your classroom. Peppered with teaching moments straight from Shane's classroom and classrooms around the nation, this book will spotlight and cultivate the teacher flame in you!

—Nicole Wong, Sixth Grade Teacher

This book, like its author, is innovative, creative, and can blaze pathways to new ideas in education. Shane's research-based ideas on building positive communities in the classroom and beyond make this book a must read for novice and veteran teachers alike.

—Megan Siclare, Third Grade Teacher

Dedication

This book is dedicated to my parents, Terri and Q, for always encouraging me to be the flame and to my partner, Ryan, for consistently supporting me to achieve my goals. I love you all.

Table of Contents

Introduction

*B*e the Flame was a phrase coined by my father and instilled in me and my siblings throughout our childhood. In short, he and my mom always encouraged us to "be the flame" in our interactions and relationships whether that meant being a strong leader or drawing others to us to have a positive impact on them. He wanted us to be the light that drew others in, like a moth to a flame, and eventually we wanted that for ourselves as well. Throughout this book you will notice a "Fire" theme, because as educators, we must all "be the flame" within our classrooms and throughout our communities. We must lead from the classroom and inspire positive interactions. As teachers, we reflect on relationships that **spark** meaning for us. We **kindle** positive rapport with students. We **ignite** a caring community among our students. We **stoke** that community to foster a culture of collaboration. We expect positive family relationships to **catch** on as meaningfully as our student relationships. We want our team relationships to **fuel** us and support us. Finally, we can leverage professional learning networks to harness an online community to **spread** and share ideas for continuous growth.

Writing this book, or any book for that matter, is an immense undertaking (especially while teaching through the COVID-19 pandemic in 2020-21). I don't take the work I've done on this book lightly. I don't consider myself a writer, but with the encouragement from many personal and professional connections and influencers, I embarked on a journey of reflection on my community-building practices as an educator. As I wrote, I found myself worrying—what if my practices and values change and evolve? I kept reminding myself that these are my practices and values *right now* and I am open to growth and change for the future. Some of these practices may be timeless and others might have an expiration date, but if we continuously grow our know-how, knowing better and doing better should become a normalized practice.

If you know me or if you've followed my teaching journey on Instagram as @fantasticallyfourth, you know that I absolutely love what I do. I love working with kids, I love piecing together engaging lessons, and I love learning and improving my craft. I am writing this book with the hope that you can take some of the ideas and activities I offer and put them into practice in your own classroom to build strong relationships with your students, among your students, and in other realms of your professional life. I am by no means an expert, but I believe in sharing experiences with others so that we can grow and learn together. Do I expect all these ideas and activities to be done with fidelity? No; that would be crazy! We are all living different experiences in different parts of the world and a one-size-fits-all approach never works—especially in education.

In the following pages you will find ideas to use in your classrooms and professional relationships to build rapport and communities in different realms of education. These relationships are the foundation to creating a safe and collaborative community environment for students and adults alike to learn, grow, and thrive in school settings. Each chapter includes a section called "Flames in the Classroom," highlighting teachers who go above and beyond with their relationship building. These phenomenal teachers each share ideas or activities that they use to build positive relationships with students, parents, teammates, and educators outside of their buildings.

I hope that these ideas spark inspiration in you to take an existing idea and make it your own: tailor it to fit the needs of your students, your classroom, and your philosophy. Take what you need, leave what you don't, but always be willing to be flexible with your thinking and open to new ideas that could impact you and your students for the better. I want this book to push educators to think about how they are building communities in their educational realm and how they can potentially dig deeper with those relationships because relationship building is the single most powerful tool educators have in their teacher toolbox.

CHAPTER 1

Spark

Teachers have the ability to *Spark* relationships that can impact students positively within the classroom.

"I've learned that people will forget what you said, people will forget what you did, but people will never forget the way you made them feel."

– Maya Angelou

When Do You Know You're an Educator?

Serving as an educator, I cannot envision myself working in any other career path. However, if you told me growing up that I would become a teacher, I would have thought you were crazy. I wasn't someone who knew that I wanted to be a teacher from a young age. I didn't teach my stuffed animals lessons or ask for a chalkboard for my birthday to hold "class." I knew I was a strong leader in many ways, but I never thought that would correlate to stepping into a profession in education.

By senior year of high school, I still hadn't figured out what I wanted to do with my life. At lunch one day it suddenly hit me: I *loved* my job working for the city in their recreational department. I ran day camps in the summer and coached sports camps during the year. I loved working with the kids in my community and being a positive role model. It brought me immense joy. It was the moment I realized that I could be a teacher and work with kids daily.

The reason I got into teaching in the first place wasn't for the academics (that passion came later), it was for the relationships. I was the student who needed a strong positive rapport with a teacher to go above and beyond. I wanted to be the teacher who inspired greatness while also helping students find it within themselves.

Upon reflection, I wanted to highlight some relationships in my own educational career that supported me as a student and shaped the type of teacher I wanted to be. I encourage you to also reflect on your own educational experiences to discover which teachers sparked your interest in learning through the relationships they built with you as a student.

Teacher "Flames" in My Educational Journey

Teacher flames are educators who work to create meaningful relationships to have a greater impact on students. Teachers who are flames in the classroom take the time to build positive rapport with students and other stakeholders to leave a positive lasting impression and impact academic outcomes. I was fortunate enough to be a student to several teachers who served as flames in my educational journey. I look back on these experiences fondly and reflect on how these teachers impacted me for the better.

In elementary school I had a third-grade teacher, Ms. Logan, who loved learning about other countries and cultures. That same year, one of my best friends and her family had the opportunity to go and live in

Australia for two months during the school year. She would be unenrolled in our class for those two months and re-enrolled once the family returned from their trip abroad.

During the time she was gone, we had our class pictures. Technically, my friend was unenrolled in our class, but Ms. Logan wanted to ensure she felt included when she returned to our class. She found a stuffed animal koala and created a small flag with my friend's name on it and tucked it into the koala's arms. She had a student hold the koala in the class picture and just like that my friend was still a part of the class photo.

The class photo could have been taken without a second thought to who was missing, but she wanted to ensure that every one of her students was included in this memory. *Ms. Logan taught me the importance of making everyone feel seen and included.*

My first day of Algebra I as a freshman in high school, I sat in the back of Mr. Welch's class as he introduced himself. He gave a presentation on success. He told us that he would not permit failure under any circumstances and that he would do everything in his power to help us succeed.

After only two weeks of Algebra I, my grade had dropped from an A to a C-. As a student growing up in the algorithm-only age of learning math, I struggled with conceptually understanding how it all worked. I was embarrassed that I did not grasp math concepts quickly and wouldn't seek out help—even if I really needed it. Mr. Welch asked me to stay after class one day to talk. He told me that he was happy to work with me during my off periods until I was back on track. The last thing I wanted to do was spend my off periods doing math work, but there was no turning back.

For the next two weeks Mr. Welch sat with me in the math tutoring lab explaining how to solve for x until it finally clicked. Mr. Welch had high expectations for all of us and he followed through on his commitment to our success. Without him reaching out and acknowledging that I needed extra support, I likely would have continued to struggle through my math classes for the rest of my educational career. *Mr. Welch taught me the importance of maintaining high expectations for all students and supporting them in reaching those expectations.*

In my junior year of high school, I blew out my knee while skiing, tearing my ACL and meniscus. I had a choir director named Mr. Ericson who was encouraging throughout my recovery which took me through the end of the school year. I was in a straight leg brace that went from the top of my quad to just above my ankle. I looked like Frankenstein with a limp walking around campus.

A week after my surgery, I returned to school on crutches and a brand-new straight leg brace. My high school was huge; it had four separate buildings and resembled a small university campus. With my crutches, it was taking me 10-15 minutes to get across campus, making me late to any class that was in a different building. I decided to ditch the crutches the following day and just hobble my way around thinking that I would be able to maneuver a little better. The only issue was that without the crutches, I was putting a lot of weight on my knee which quickly became painful.

One day, by sixth period I was exhausted, in excruciating pain, and frustrated at my inability to keep up. I hobbled into the choir room and Mr. Ericson must have noticed something was wrong (I have literally zero poker face). As soon as he asked if I was okay, I burst into tears. He directed me into his office and told me to take some time to myself and he'd be in to check on me. He let me know that if I ever needed a space in the school to breathe and take a moment for myself that his door was always open.

Mr. Ericson is an incredibly kind soul and *I learned from him that compassion and empathy for your students can go a long way to building trust and a safe space in which to learn and grow.*

My junior year of college was the year that I met Dr. Shelby Wolf, who taught the children's literature class for the school of education.

Our first assignment was to read a picture book of our choice and use visual components to showcase the plot of the story. In the directions, it said that drawing, painting, dioramas, and clip art could be used. The picture book I chose was *Lon PoPo*, a Red-Riding Hood story from China. Unfortunately, I was still in the habit of finishing assignments with the least amount of work possible. I saw the words "clip art" and threw together some images onto a Word document. I printed it out and brought it to class.

When I arrived, I looked around at all the beautiful visuals that had been created by my peers and immediately felt sheepish. There were watercolor paintings, pastel drawings, detailed sketches, clay dioramas—and then, there was my clip art page. She walked around looking at the finished products. When she passed mine, all she did was give me a quizzical look and kept walking. She went on to explain that in true elementary fashion, our work was going to be displayed outside the classroom on the bulletin board for everyone in the education department to see.

As class ended, Shelby asked me to stay after and chat. She asked if I was proud of my work. I immediately said no and that I had misinterpreted the magnitude of the assignment. She said that it was all right and there would be many other assignments to make up for it, but that it was a good lesson to always put your best foot forward. *From Dr. Wolf, I learned the importance of always inspiring your students to want to do their best work.*

Another amazing woman I met on my educational journey was Dr. Donna Begley, who I was lucky enough to learn from while earning both my undergraduate and my first graduate degree. Dr. Begley was one of the most beloved professors in the School of Education. During my first semester in the School of Education I took an Integrated Reading course with Donna. One of our big assignments for the semester was to pick a grade and 3-5 standards from that grade around which to create activities. After the clip art fiasco, I knew that these professors were not going to let us slide by with subpar work. I carefully chose four standards to build activities around. I can't remember all the activities, but I remember creating a card game that allowed students to practice identifying facts versus opinions and a sorting game where students had to apply their comprehension of a story to put events in sequential order. I remember Donna coming to my table as I walked my group through each of the activities. When I was finished, she told me my activities were fantastic and that I had done a great job on this project. It was such a small moment, but it made me want to work hard and continue to improve. I *wanted* to put my best foot forward to be the best educator I could be. *Donna taught me that even the smallest of conversations and affirmations to students can leave lasting impacts.*

Finally, in my undergraduate program, I had the opportunity to take a differentiation class with Dr. Sue Hopewell. In my final semester before student teaching, I had filmed a whole group lesson in my practicum classroom for an assignment. I was excited about how engaged the students were, how many different volunteers had shared out, and how well the lesson had gone overall.

I went to rewatch my lesson later and at first, everything seemed great. However, I noticed that one of the students in the back of the class had started picking their nose in the video. Then, a little bit of blood was coming from the first grader's nose and instead of going to get a tissue, she proceeded to stick all ten fingers into the bloody nose. To my horror, she started playfully clawing at other students in the back row.

I was beside myself. How could this student have picked their nose until it was bloody, proceeded to stick all ten of her fingers in the blood, playfully claw at other students in the back of the class, and I didn't notice this happening at all? I was too embarrassed to submit this video. Would they think that I had poor classroom management? I had Sue's class the following day and decided I would ask her opinion about what I should do.

I showed Sue the video and as she watched the video, she let out a laugh and then told me not to worry. We don't always see everything going on in the classroom, but it was a good learning experience to be aware of everything that is happening in the room. Then, she shared her own experience during her first-year teaching. Her principal had walked into her classroom for her very first observation and she was so nervous and focused on executing the lesson with precision that she didn't notice when a fist fight broke out in the back of the room and her principal was the one who had to break it up. I was so relieved that I wasn't the only one this had happened to.

Sue taught me that bringing an understanding lens to our interactions with students and even sharing a similar experience with them is a powerful tool. These help us build and cultivate connections, allow students to feel safe, and promote their growth.

There are many moments, both big and small, that go into creating rapport and relationships between students and teachers. I chose to reflect on small, specific moments that resonated and stuck with me. However, rapport isn't built in one interaction, it's built over many interactions. It's important that we reflect on our own experiences as well as the experiences we have with our students to increase our capacity for building positive relationships and communities in our classrooms. Reflection is one of the most powerful tools an educator can use in their practice to become more effective. I hope you're able to take some important tidbits from your own educational past to infuse into your own craft.

> Reflection is one of the most powerful tools an educator can use in their practice to become more effective.

Be the Flame Actions

Think about the teacher(s) who had a significant and positive impact on you as a learner and complete the following:

- Make a list of influential teachers in your life and reflect on:
  - How did the teacher(s) make you feel as a student in their classroom?
  - What did the teacher(s) do to build positive rapport?
- Choose 1-2 practices that these teachers used to build rapport and make a plan to integrate them into your own practice.

CHAPTER 2

Kindle

Teachers must work to *Kindle* one-on-one
relationships with their students to encourage
them to do and be their absolute best.

"Every child deserves a champion—an adult who will never give up
on them, who understands the power of connection and insists that
they become the best that they can possibly be. "
– Rita F. Pierson

Building Positive Relationships

Many education books, especially books referencing how to kick off the beginning of the year, discuss the importance of building positive relationships with students. These positive relationships can help with classroom management, engagement, motivation, and so much more. Although we all agree how important positive relationships with students are, it can be difficult to find explicit ways to build those one-on-one relationships.

On my Instagram account, I often receive direct messages from other teachers who wonder how to handle different management situations or ask what management strategies I use in the classroom to have such consistent participation and on-task behavior. I always tell them that it comes down to the positive relationships I've built with students. This foundation of rapport is the backbone of my entire classroom management approach—and recently I've come to dislike the word "management" to describe how I run my classroom. I don't ever feel as if I am "managing" my kids. I feel that our mutual respect allows us to depend on one another, engage in tasks together, and comply when necessary out of mutual respect.

In one of my education-based TikTok videos, I shared a clip of a writing lesson that I completed with my class. Someone commented, "What is the purpose behind calling them 'friend'? Don't you think it's dangerous for them to see you as a friend and not an authority figure?" This question blew my mind because I don't see myself as an authority figure. I ended up responding to the comment, "Friend is gender neutral (inclusive). I am not an authority figure—we build a relationship of mutual respect, not hierarchy." Although teachers are seemingly authoritative, in the end, we have no power if students are not willing to work with us and complete their best work in safe environments in which they feel comfortable and cared for. This is why relationships are so important to me as an educator: they are the foundation to a successful classroom.

In her well-known TED Talk, Rita Pierson states that students don't learn from teachers they don't like. I find this to be true. Even in my own experience as a student, I felt this way. The teachers who had not taken the time to grow a relationship with me did not receive my best work. If I felt that my teachers did not care about me as an individual, I in turn, did not care much about their class or content. We are our best selves around people who encourage us to work hard and in environments in which we feel safe to take risks. Children are no exception to this. Relationships are a critical component to students feeling comfortable in the classroom and they need safe environments cultivated by teachers to excel.

> We are our best selves around people who encourage us to work hard and in environments in which we feel safe to take risks.

Teachers who build positive relationships with students will find that these relationships can extend beyond the time spent with them in a single school year. These strong positive relationships with students create an environment in which students feel successful and want to keep in touch down the road. It's fulfilling to still be in contact with multiple students and families from previous years because of the strong-rooted relationships we created. Past students might come in and volunteer in the classroom on their days off or send letters or emails giving an update on their lives. It's those moments, when I receive a letter or email out of the blue from a past student, when I realize that even all this time later they want to reach out and connect. The strong bonds that are forged over the course of a year have the potential to be long lasting—and they remind us that we are truly making a difference, even if only in incremental steps.

Relationship Building Ideas

In any education book you read or class you take, the importance of building relationships with students is stressed: relationships over everything, relationships before content, and relationships are key to a successful school year. I knew that relationships were important, but I felt that other than a few ice breaker activities, I wasn't prepared with more ideas on how to continue building rapport with students. What follows are concrete ideas for you to use in your classroom to build relationships with your students. You can implement these strategies at any point in the year—it's never too late to build on those connections:

Learning names on the first day of school - Knowing students' names should be a priority on the first day of school. It shows students that you honor who they are as individuals and know it's important to know who they are. I usually play a name game (I'll give some ideas below) and after the name game I ask if they think that I can go around the room and name every student. They don't usually think I can do it, but I have yet to mess up. It helps that I have my roster a few days before school starts and label supplies in the classroom with their names, but they don't have to know that!

It's also incredibly important that we learn to pronounce student names properly. If you're unsure how to pronounce a student name—ask! Ask them to pronounce it, tell them you are working on making sure you pronounce it correctly because it's important, and then practice saying their name. Names are important; there is often a story or meaning behind each one. We want our students to feel like they belong and that we see them as individuals.

If a student wants to use a preferred name, let them; it's their identity. For example, my father goes by "Q" as his first name. It's the equivalent of the Iranian nickname for his birth name. Even when he specifically asks to be called by Q, there are some who still ask for his birth name pronunciation. He has created his individual identity around the name Q and doesn't feel connected to his birth name. It is more respectful to him to call him by his preferred name than his birth name because that is what he desires.

That being said, make sure that you never ask to *give* a student a nickname because you have a hard time pronouncing their name. It's our job as educators to put the work into pronouncing student names correctly to show that we respect them as individuals.

Name Game Ideas:

Alliteration Name Game - Students say their name and something they like or do that starts with the same sound as their name.

Add On Name Game - I saw this used in a prim[...]
where a student would say their name and do a "m[...]
son next to them would say the friend's name be[...]
move, then say their own name, and do a move of [...]
students, they could try and remember all the nam[...] [...] [...]
go around the circle.

Remember Me Name Game - Students introduce themselves and then introduce the one person that went before them. This way, names are being said multiple times. NOTE: the student who goes first will just introduce themselves. You can add things into this, like having students say their name and something they like to do.

Explain Your Name: I participated in this recently in my doctoral class. You tell the story behind your name, middle name, and/or last name. The stories are always quite interesting.

After learning all students' names and how to pronounce them correctly, it is time to delve deeper into learning more about them as people. Here are some other ideas to consider:

Cultural artifact - The cultural artifact activity is one of my favorite activities to do during the first few days together in the classroom. This is a great way to get to know students on a deeper level and engage in sharing something that is important to them. The cultural artifact activity is similar to show and tell as students bring something from home to share with the class. However, here is the catch: It must be something meaningful to them that shows their culture. Some students might say, "Well, I don't have a culture," but *everyone* has a culture. Encourage students to talk with their families about traditions that are unique to their family—that is culture right there. I love how students can come in with an item that represents something about their culture and share more about their family, heritage, and/or traditions in which they take part.

Before sending them home to talk with their family and find a culture artifact, I model a couple of artifacts that represent different parts of my culture. First, I share a piece of fluorine with them that represents my Iranian heritage. I explain that my family is from Iran and when they lived in Iran, they owned a mine that extracted fluorine and this was a piece from that very mine. I also explain that my family had to flee from Iran to the United States for safety during the revolution and that my father and his family are immigrants. I explain that this fluorine is important to me because it reminds me of where I am from and of my family who did everything they could so that my siblings and I could have the opportunities we have today.

Another item I model with is an ornament that hangs in my classroom. It reads: "When it's raining look for rainbows, when it's dark look for stars." I explain that this item is important to me because my mother gave it to me when I was having a hard time in college. A friend I was very close with moved away and I was missing her a lot. I go on to explain that my family is very close, and we are always there to support one another. It reminds me that even when things seem hard or scary, that there are better times to come on the other side.

I make sure that I front load this activity by communicating with my students' families, letting them know that this is something their child is coming home to talk with them about. I ask students to take a night or two and choose an item to bring in and tell the class about and I give them a sheet with these questions to fill out and have prepared:

1. What is your artifact?
2. Did someone special give it to you? If so, who?
3. Did you get your artifact in a special place? If so, where?
4. Why is this artifact important to you?
5. What memory comes to mind when you look at your artifact?
6. Anything else you would like to share about your artifact?

The items and stories that students share show so much of who they are, where they come from, what they value, who their families are, and so much more. Not only does it help you get to know your students, but it also helps your students get to know one another, too. I've seen this activity employed from first grade all the way through sixth grade—students love the opportunity to bring in a special item and talk about why it's special.

Quality time - Spending non-academic time with students is a great way to get to know their hobbies or interests outside of school. You can also find things that you have in common with your students to bond over and discuss throughout the year. You'll find that students become very excited when you spend time with them outside of class. They open up and sometimes you see the goofy social side that you may not see in the classroom.

At times, I realize that I watch some of the same TV series on Disney+ as my students (Mandolorian, anyone?) or read the same book series and talk about what they thought of the characters or ending. These small touch points can make all the difference in building rapport and connecting with your students.

Lunch in the Cafeteria: I like to take at least one lunch a week and spend it eating in the cafeteria with the kids. The first time you do this, they'll be so surprised that you're going to eat with them. I usually hear, "Seriously, Ms. Saeed, you're going to eat with us?! Can you sit with me?"

During this time, I like to ask about what they did that weekend, what they have coming up that they're excited about, or what is new and popular that I should know about (this question comes with some hilarious answers and then the reminder that I'm getting older and no longer young and hip *sigh*). Sometimes I like to tell cheesy jokes and see if students can "out cheese" me—this may or may not be where I pick up some of my favorite jokes. Just in case you need some cheesy jokes to start you off, here are some of my favorites:

1. What do you call a pig that does karate? (A pork chop!)
2. Have you heard the joke about the pencil? (I better not tell you; you may not get the point!)
3. Why does a bike need a kickstand? (Because it's two-tired!)
4. Why can't you hear a pterodactyl go to the bathroom? (Because the "p" is silent!)

Recess: Going out and playing with students at recess can help twofold: you can build relationships through shared activities *and* increase your own endorphin levels through some movement and being outside—it's a win-win. I grew up playing soccer, so I have a great time getting out onto the field and playing with my students.

Other games I love to play include "Knock Out" on the basketball court, which is a blast because you don't have to know how to play basketball to play—anyone can join in. In case you're unfamiliar, Knock Out is played with two basketballs and has no limit on players. The object of the game is to score a basket before the person ahead of you in line scores in order to knock them out of the game. Everyone lines up single file behind the free throw line and the first two players in line start with the basketballs. The first player has to shoot the ball before the second player can shoot. If the second player scores before the first player, the first player is out and both balls are passed to the third and fourth players in line to start again. However, if the first player scores first, they pass their ball to the third player and go to the back of the line to keep playing. Now, the third player is trying to make it in before the second player. This cycle keeps going until there are only two players left trying to knock one another out.

Infection tag is also a lot of fun and has been huge at my school for years. It's another game anyone can play. There is one person who is the

20

original tagger who is "infected" and anyone they tag becomes "infected" and a tagger as well. Just a general warning: if you play tag with your students, expect to run because you will be target number one.

Not all students like to run around at recess and it's important to include them, too. I like to buy big buckets of chalk to draw on the sidewalk with students. Anyone can draw pictures, hopscotch, decorate their name, etc. Swinging with students and simply talking is another great activity to do with kids who do not wish to run around. I highly recommend engaging in a mixture of activities throughout the year so that you're spending time with all your students.

Lunch Bunches: If your school allows you to, invite your entire class to lunch bunches in your classroom. This is where students can eat their lunches in your room. Eating in the classroom is exciting within itself, but you can add other things in to make it even more fun. Sometimes, they get to pick the songs we listen to (Kidz Bop, of course) or we watch Kid Snippets on YouTube which are video clips where the audio is of younger kids telling stories and adults acting out the audio. They are hilarious! Other ideas include a board game lunch bunch, a book club lunch bunch where everyone listens to an audiobook of their choosing, or even a passion project lunch bunch where students engage in long term projects or research of their choice. The possibilities are endless.

Checking In with students - Having systems to check in on how students are doing individually is important. Teaching can be hectic and when a student is struggling, they may or may not be showing signs that they need some more support. There are times we can spot when a student is feeling a little off because their behavior has deviated from their norm, but there are also many times when students may be struggling in silence and having an open-door policy isn't enough. Giving students different avenues to communicate with you can help them advocate for themselves in a way that feels comfortable to them.

Sticky Note Check-In: Sticky note check-ins are simple and easy to implement. I love these check-ins because they can be done at a moment's notice. All you need is a sticky note for each student and to write a few sentence stems on the board for them to complete on their sticky note. I have them put their number on their sticky note (each student is given a number at the beginning of the year for organizational purposes) to help keep their note anonymous as they turn it in. I ask the students to complete the following sentence stems:

1. I feel _____.
2. I wonder _____.
3. I need _____.

You will be surprised by how open students can be. Some students will let you know they're happy and don't need anything, while others may let you know that they're feeling down and may need some extra breaks throughout the day. I've had students advocate for more help with a math skill they don't feel confident about yet or wanting a book recommendation. It's amazing the information you can receive if you give them opportunities to express themselves.

To use this with younger students, think about using pictures or emoji faces for them to respond to the "I feel..." sentence stem. You can draw a variety of faces on the board for them to use (smiley face, sad face, indifferent face) or leave it open ended. For any student who reports a sad or indifferent face you can check in with them, having a quick conversation to see how they are.

Weekly Feedback Form: Like many teachers around the globe, the COVID-19 pandemic forced me to teach virtually. GoogleDoc feedback forms have been a lifesaver in the virtual environment. I send a GoogleDoc out to students via our Learning Management System (We use Schoology for this) each week and they type their answers to the same questions each week. I use the following questions to help them reflect:

1. What did you do well this week?
2. What would you like to improve on for next week?
3. What was something you liked this week?
4. What was something you didn't like this week?
5. Do you have any questions or feedback for me?

It may be scary as a teacher to ask your students what they didn't like about the week, but I've come to the conclusion that I would rather know. If there is an activity they didn't like, I can stop using it or work with them to figure out how to change it to something they enjoy. It's also important that I know what they enjoyed so that I can continue to use activities that are highly engaging. Student agency increases engagement and by listening to your students and implementing their feedback and using it to help make decisions moving forward, you are giving your students a voice in the classroom. This helps to build community and trust between you and your students.

When I started using this system, I realized that I had helped open a door of communication between a few of my students who are quiet and don't feel comfortable speaking up about their needs. One student used the form to let me know that she was uncomfortable using the type of seat that she was using in her small group. The following Monday, I touched base with her to lay out some choices for her to try and we found one that was a much better option. Without the GoogleDoc, she may not have mentioned anything and would have been uncomfortable the rest of the year.

I had another student who was particularly quiet and new to the school. The second week back in school, she used her feedback document to mention that she noticed we were getting down to lunch 3-5 minutes late each day which made it difficult for her to get through the lunch line and finish her food since students only get twenty minutes to eat. The following Monday, I thanked her for her feedback and told her I would make sure we got down to lunch on time. I started setting timers for myself so that we were able to clean up and transition across the building right on time for their lunch. By doing this, I wanted to show that I knew "their time" was just as important as "my time." Had this student not brought this concern to my attention, we would probably have continued to get to lunch 3-5 minutes late and she would have felt rushed every single day.

Feedback from students can be daunting because inherently we want to think everything is going well. However, without feedback we cannot change our practice. Receiving feedback is critical to changing our practice for the better and we cannot let our pride get in the way of giving students a voice in the classroom.

> Receiving feedback is critical to changing our practice for the better and we cannot let our pride get in the way of giving students a voice in the classroom.

Individual Check-In Book: As educators, we know that differentiation in the classroom is fundamental to helping all students succeed. There are students for whom a weekly GoogleDoc or Sticky Note Check-In isn't enough. In the past, I've had a few students who needed a medium for daily communication with me on how they were feeling and if they needed a one-on-one check-in to talk. I made these students "Check-In Books" out of blank books I found at the Target Dollar Spot (the dollar section located in the front of Target stores). I glue in response pages for them to fill out either during independent work time or in the morning when we are settling in. Once they finish, they can hand it to me or place it on my rolling cart to read. The sentence stems on each page include:

Today I'm feeling _____ because
_____.

I wish my teacher knew _____
_____.

I (circle one: DO / DON'T) need to check in and talk. If you circled DO:

I would like to check in about _____
_____.

This gives my more introverted students who need more support the opportunity to connect with me directly each day, let me know how they are doing, and whether they need extra support from me. Again, it's providing students multiple ways to communicate their needs with you. This helps build trust and positive rapport with students who need help feeling seen and heard.

Flames in the Classroom #1:

Jillian Starr

Jillian is a second-grade teacher in Boston, Massachusetts. Here, Jillian shares a way that she builds relationships with her students through journaling:

When looking to build rapport with students, we need to make a conscious effort to learn about them as individuals. Yet because teachers often find they do not have any time to spare during the day, it can feel like an insurmountable task to deeply engage each student in your classroom individually.

One way that I've found to truly get to know my students is by making one of my literacy centers each week a "journaling" center. Each student gets their own journal, and it hosts a conversation between the two of us. There are no requirements or expectations; students are free to write whatever is on their hearts and minds. They can tell me about their soccer game, what was hard for them in school that week, something that has been bothering them on the playground, or that they miss a parent who might be traveling or working evening shifts.

The lack of structure in this activity allows my students to tell me what's important to them, not what *we* think is important to them. This is critical because we, as adults, often think we know what information will help us earn trust and lay the groundwork of our relationships with our students. However, allowing them to initiate the conversations allows us to take their lead, which I believe not only builds trust more quickly, but also establishes a strong foundation on which to build a relationship.

I believe the power of this kind of journaling lies in the fact that writing allows students a safe place to share intimate details about their world, without the pressure of a face-to-face conversation. Students can take their time, decide how they want to word their ideas, add pictures, and erase if they decide they've shared something that they would like to take back. To ensure that each of my students is able to access this activity, modifications are always in place for students who struggle with written output. My goal is for my students to share, and if handwriting is going to be an obstacle, we work together to decide what accommodations will work best to make sure they can.

My favorite part about this type of journaling is writing back to students. Yes, I write back to each student, and my response is directly related to what they share. I often share a personal connection I made with their writing or ask follow up questions. When they share successes, I make sure to celebrate those wins with them in my responses. When they trust me enough to share an issue they're having, I take the opportunity to validate their feelings and follow up with a checklist of options we could use to begin problem-solving. My students cannot wait to get their journals back once they know I've responded, in order to continue with our conversation.

A final important detail is that I tell my students these journals will only ever be seen by the two of us unless they choose otherwise. I have students put a smiley face at the top of entries they are comfortable with me sharing outside of our written conversation. This might include sharing at conferences with caregivers, or with specialist teachers. If there is no smiley face, I assume the conversation is to be kept private, and I respect those wishes.

Building individual rapport with students is best done when we allow it to start with them and follow them wherever they're willing to take us.

Connect with Jillian:
Instagram: @jillianstarrteaching
Twitter: @jillianteaching
Website: JillianStarrTeaching.com

Attention-getters - Attention-getters are one of my favorite and quickest ways to build relationships. If you aren't familiar, attention-getters are call and response activities that teachers use with students to call their attention to them. The teacher calls out a known phrase, students respond with a phrase, and then they give you their full attention. I start the year by introducing some of my favorite attention-getters—most of which I learned through day camp counseling for the YMCA and through the *Get Your Teach On* (GYTO) conference. Some of my favorites include the following:

Finding Nemo Attention-Getter, Wade King, GYTO:
Teacher: Shark bait!
Students: Woo-Ha-Ha! *clap*

Toy Story Attention-Getter, Hope King, GYTO:
Teacher: Andy's coming!
Students: *Students freeze as if they were toys*
Teacher: Coast is clear!
Students: *Clap pattern of your choice*

YMCA Attention-Getter:
Teacher: Hey, hey, hey listen up, listen up!
Students: *repeat back* Hey, hey, hey listen up, listen up!

YMCA Attention-Getter:
Teacher: Take a seat, take a seat, take a load off your feet!
Students: What, what!

Call and response created by me to release students after an attention getter:
Teacher: **gives directions** Get it?
Students: Got it!
Teacher: Good! Go!

Once I introduce these attention-getters, I let my students know that I would like them to keep adding to the attention-getters. They love coming up with attention-getters and being able to share them and the look on their faces when you use their attention-getter for the first time is priceless! Again, bringing in student agency in this small way can be a great way to build relationships with your students.

Here are just a few of my favorite attention-getters that students have contributed over the years:

Teacher: All hail the queen!
Students: Yas, queen!

Teacher: Gotta catch 'em all!
Students: Pokemon!

Teacher: Red Robin!
Students: Yummmm!

Teacher: Dino!
Students: RAWR! *Makes T-Rex arms*

Teacher: Animal crackers in my...
Students: soup! *clap*

Teacher: Who lives in a pineapple under the sea?
Students: Spongebob Square Pants!

Morning greetings and afternoon goodbyes - Starting the day with a smile and being acknowledged by name can help start a student's day off on the right foot. I greet each student by name and with a smile every morning. Students can choose how they would like to be greeted. They can choose a hug, high five, fist bump, handshake, or wave each morning. I use a product I found on Teachers Pay Teachers from the Core Coaches where each greeting has a visual that is posted outside my classroom. This way, students can point to how they would like to be greeted.

I thought it was important to have a variety of ways to greet students. Sometimes, students are more comfortable with waving than they are with a hug or high five. Choices are important; again, giving agency to students regarding how they are greeted is a great way to build trust.

Every morning, when I am outside my classroom greeting students, it sounds like this:

"Good morning, _____!" with a big smile on my face and using the greeting action of their choice.

Every afternoon we follow the same routine. Students line up in the classroom, and one by one they choose the way they would like to say goodbye. It sounds like this:

"Bye, _____! Have a great day!" with a smile on my face and using the goodbye action of their choice.

Just like we want to start the day on a high note, we want to send them home feeling warm and fuzzy, too. When they get back to their families, we want them to be happy and feel seen. In other classrooms, I've seen student and teacher greetings in other fun ways. My teammate loves llamas, and her class greets each other in the morning by making a llama head with their hands (middle and ring finger touching the thumb) and "bowing" to one another. I've also seen teachers who create handshakes with each of their students and do the handshake while greeting them in the morning and saying goodbye in the afternoon.

My first year teaching I had the students simply file in as they got to the door and when the bell rang, they lined up and walked out on their own. Being intentional with my greetings and goodbyes wasn't a practice I started until my third year (I'm a bit embarrassed to admit that), but there was a noticeable difference in student readiness to start the day and how happy they were as they left in the afternoon. It small things like greetings and goodbyes that make a huge differenc and should be a staple in all classrooms.

Bring in student ideas - Be open to accepting lesson or activity ideas from your students. If they have an idea for a review game, reading activity, math game, etc. hear them out and figure out if there is a way to work it into your classroom plans.

There is a two-fold effect from doing this. First, the student whose idea it was will be incredibly excited that you're using their idea for a lesson. They will be beaming with pride the entire time. Second, announcing to your class that this was another student's idea will let them know that you're open to their ideas and get them thinking about ways they can contribute to the classroom too.

I had a student who was having a hard time collaborating with his group. He didn't want to engage in the work and because of that, he didn't want to work with his teammates. Math was hard and building up his confidence was a slow process. One day, this same student came to me with a math game idea. He described a game in which students do math problems and for every correct answer, they earn a part of a stick figure, ultimately creating a stickman. The team to make their stickman first, wins. I loved this idea and thought it would be easy enough to implement. I asked him if it was okay if I changed a couple of small details such as making it a collaborative group activity instead of individual and if we could focus on working as a team rather than winning. He agreed and the next day I introduced it.

I explained to the students that as they worked through their book-work in their collaborative teams (collaborative teams are explained further in Chapter 4) that they would have to get each problem they finished checked by me. If every member had the correct work and answer on their page, they would earn a part of their stickman. We have a positivity chart in our room (where clips only ever go up, not down)

ımulate points to earn them long-term incentives.
ollaborate well with their group, the team would
ıd if they finished their stickman, they could clip
:y were all so excited to play Stickman and when I
s a certain student's idea, they congratulated him
on the great idea. After the math block was finished, there was a lot of
buzz about how much fun they had playing Stickman and they gave
the student a round of applause for coming up with such a great idea. It
was heart-warming to see them be
so excited for another student.

After recess, the student whose
idea it was approached me with a
note. It said:"Dear Ms. Saeed, I love
my group. I love teamwork. Thanks
for making the Stickman project
possible." Just by integrating his
idea, I helped to create an environment in which he wanted to work
with his team and wanted to engage
in the math work. The power of student agency is incredibly strong
and can reach students who may be disengaged or indifferent towards
their learning.

> The power of student agency is incredibly strong and can reach students who may be disengaged or indifferent towards their learning.

Positive to negative interaction ratio - In every classroom there are
going to be times when we need to redirect a student. However, we
also need to think about ensuring that for every negative interaction,
we have at least two positive interactions (Hammond, 2015). If we
are consistently redirecting a student without giving them any positive
feedback, what message does that send to them? A negative interaction
could be correcting their work, redirecting their behavior, or telling
them that their actions were not meeting expectations. Positive interactions are considered praise or affirmations. Another important thing

to note is that your positive interaction wit
individualized; you cannot praise the class a
a student feels individually praised. Students
individually for the positive interaction to be r

    One year, I had a student who was distanci
the class. I noticed that he had stopped makin
hood in the classroom, and was even more quiet ....y was.
I wanted to reach out to him but felt that reaching out directly would
make him even more uncomfortable. That's when I started reflecting on
all our interactions in the past week. Almost all our recent interactions
involved me redirecting him in some way. Even if it was well-meaning
and in a kind tone, redirecting a student is pointing out that they're
doing something incorrectly or unexpected. The message I was sending
to him was loud and clear: You aren't doing anything right. I made the
conscious effort to ensure I was praising and affirming him the following week because he typically exhibited expected behavior 90% of the
time, but I was only ever pointing out the 10%. I thanked him for his
hard work in math, I praised him for getting in line quickly and quietly,
I praised him for being on task and listening during mini lessons, and
so on. By the end of the week, the hood had come off and the eye contact was back.

    If you're struggling with your relationship with a student, reflect
on your interactions and what your ratio might be. Make an effort to
praise or affirm the student *at least* two times for every time you have
to redirect them.

Creating Expectations with Your Students

Following the theme of student agency, creating classroom expectations
collaboratively with your students is another powerful tool for students
to feel seen and heard by their teacher. Instead of unilaterally imposing
our expectations on students, having them discuss and create a set of

to abide by allows them to have a voice and an investment that is expected of them in the classroom. Each year that I do this, students create the same—if not better—rules for themselves than I would have created by myself. Students value an environment in which they are safe and respected. Below is how I implement this process in my classroom:

1. I ask students to independently reflect for one minute on rules they believe are important in the classroom.
2. I then have them discuss what rules they think are important and why they are important in a small group of two or three students for two minutes.
3. Next, I ask students to share out all the rules they think are important to follow in the classroom and I write them all down on the white board. This usually takes about five to seven minutes.
4. I then introduce the term "umbrella rule" to students, explaining that a lot of these rules can be covered under one larger "umbrella" rule. For example, "Treat others the way you want to be treated" and "Use your words kindly" can both be covered under the umbrella rule "Be respectful."
5. Together, we look for commonalities among the rules they have come up with to create umbrella rules that can encompass similar concepts. Typically, the broad umbrella rules fall under categories such as: be respectful, be safe, be responsible, and be positive.
6. Once we decide on four to five umbrella rules that we are going to abide by, I write them down on a rules poster. Then, students sign their name to the rules, agreeing to follow them.

Having classroom rules that are student created gives students a sense of empowerment and ownership over those expectations. If a student feels like a peer isn't meeting expectations, you'll hear them remind each other of the class rules. It also makes redirecting behavior easier. Rather than tell a student that something wasn't respectful, I might ask them if they were following the class rules they created and agreed to follow. Usually, they take ownership of their actions and redirect themselves. It's an easy way to give agency to your students at the beginning of the year that will pay dividends throughout the year.

The Power of One-on-One Conversations

Whenever I post on social media platforms about flexible learning spaces, big room transformations, or working in collaborative groups, I get the same question: "What happens when a student won't follow the expectations?" I tell them that I usually have a one-on-one conversation with the student and that usually does the trick—and, inevitably, the person asking the question is stunned. A conversation can change behavior? Yes, it can!

One-on-one conversations can be used in a variety of ways. They can be used to help redirect student behavior or to affirm student behavior. For example, I had a student who was working on not becoming overly physical at recess when he became upset while playing football. As I watched the students play, I could see that this student was becoming more and more irritated with his team. Finally, I heard him yell at his team and walk away. I called him over and I could tell he was waiting for me to reprimand him for his behavior. On the contrary, I praised him for not getting physical and instead walking away from the situation. I also acknowledged that the yelling may not have been the best choice, but that is something we can continue to work on together. I told him I was proud of him for not letting his escalated state get the better of him. The power of that private, individual conversation paid off because he assumed true ownership of his reactions at recess following our conversation.

I also use individual conversations when I need to redirect the behavior of a specific student. I start the conversation by pointing out the actions I've observed (make sure it's not about emotion). I remind the student of my expectations and ask if they met those expectations. When they take ownership of their actions, we create an action plan listing things the student can do to ensure their success moving forward. This way, the student has something tangible that they can immediately begin working on. At the end of any conversation during which I redirect a student, I remind them that making a bad choice does not make them a bad person and that I love and care for them. This last part is the most important because students can internalize these conversations as us thinking that they are inherently "bad," which is not the case at all. It's critical that they hear from us that they are a good person and that we still love and care for them.

Apologizing to Students

We may be adults, but that does not mean we are always right. Teachers make mistakes, too. If we are wrong and it impacts a student, an apology can go a long way toward repairing that relationship. I remember a student who told me that she had turned in an assignment—spoiler alert: she had. I was pretty positive that I had not seen her assignment and asked her to look in her folder again. It still wasn't there so we looked through every single folder and notebook in her desk and we still couldn't find it. Finally, I rechecked the stack of turned-in assignments and found her assignment tucked into the middle.

I felt awful for asking her to continue to look when she had already turned in the assignment. I looked her right in the eyes and told her how sorry I was for asking her to recheck and said that I should have checked my own stack first before asking her to look through everything in her desk. She looked at me stunned and said it was all right. I asked why she seemed surprised, and she said that she didn't usually hear teachers say they made a mistake. That moment was meaningful to me in showing how powerful it can be to apologize when we are wrong. Take it from me, don't let those small moments pass you by. The vulnerability you show in those moments helps you to continue to build trust with your students.

How Positive Relationships Help Students Succeed

I want to leave you with a story close to my heart which illustrates why I truly believe that building strong personal relationships with students is one of the most powerful tools you can have in your teacher toolbox. You cannot control what adversities or experiences a student is having outside of school, but you can create a safe environment for them to thrive in for the seven hours you spend with them five days a week. We, as teachers, sometimes spend more time with our students than they do with their own families. It's important that we use our time wisely with them.

One year, I had a student who was having a hard time regulating his emotions at the beginning of the year. There were changes happening at his home and the transition back into a school schedule was proving to be a lot for him. He would "elope," which means running out of my classroom unexpectedly, or tell me that he was bad, and I should just call his parents. Behavior is a form of communication, and this student was trying to tell me something. He was not bad, he was not disrespectful, he was not giving me a hard time. He was having a hard time and asking for help.

One day, after eloping from my classroom, I asked the administrator who was following the student if she would watch my class while I talked with the student. The administrator agreed and I sat down next to the student in the hallway and asked how he was feeling. Then, I just listened. He talked about how he didn't like school because one of his parents told him that he was only reading at a third-grade level and he took that to mean he was a bad reader. I let him finish and told him that he was a much better reader than he thought. I explained to the student that he was a good reader, but we'd work together to help him become an even better reader. All his actions came down to his insecurity about his reading and disappointing his parents. That small conversation was the start to building a relationship that would help this student succeed, not just academically, but socially and emotionally as well.

Be the Flame Actions

Reflect on how you have built relationships with students from past years and consider the following:

- How have I built relationships in the past? What were the most effective relationship-building techniques?
- Choose one activity mentioned in this chapter to do with your own students.
- Identify a student that you could have an even stronger relationship with and track your negative to positive ratio—see if the positives are outweighing the negatives.
- If the opportunity presents itself, have a one-on-one conversation with a student to help redirect them. Don't forget to mention that you love and care about them at the end of the conversation!

CHAPTER 3

Ignite

As teachers, it is our job to *Ignite* a powerful
community in our classrooms where students work
together and support one another.

"The greatness of a community is most accurately measured by the
compassionate actions of its members."
— Coretta Scott King

Building Community among the Students
in Your Classroom

You wouldn't know it from watching me talk on Instagram stories, but speaking in front of people I do not know or feel comfortable with is hard for me. I can talk to a room full of students or make a story on Instagram that thousands of people might view, but I still have a hard time speaking up in professional development events or classes for fear of being wrong or judged. I think most people can relate to this feeling, but it's not a feeling I want my students to worry about. Through my own experience as both a student and educator, I understand the importance of creating a space where it's safe to be wrong and share without judgement.

Normalize Mistakes

In my classroom, I am constantly reminding students that they should speak up and share their ideas, even when they are unsure of their answers. I like to remind them that making mistakes can be *good* because mistakes often help us learn. I go so far as to point out the mistakes I make in front of them to normalize it—and if they can catch a mistake of mine that is even better. I thank them for pointing it out and move to correct it. Recently, I was teaching a math lesson and working through a multi-step word problem with my class and made not one, not two, but three mistakes as I worked through the problem. I thought I was ready to move on to the next step when a little voice said, "Um, Ms. Saeed, that's not what I got…" followed by a chorus of "Me either!" My focus was not on the problem at hand, and it showed, but I had a group of students who were delighted to kindly tell me I had made a mistake. I love that they felt comfortable enough to stop me and correct me, I love that they corrected me kindly, I love that they saw I am human, too.

I shared this small moment out on Instagram and received a lot of wonderful feedback about normalizing mistakes. However, I had one teacher state that they like to say, "Good, I'm glad you saw the mistake I made on purpose to see if you were paying attention." I've thought long and hard about this comment and I've concluded that if we, as teachers, are playing our mistakes off as being "on purpose" we are setting a precedent that we are always right and know all—which is certainly not the case. We are a very vital part of creating a classroom learning community. As educators, we have the incredible opportunity to model learning behaviors, problem solving, being wrong, and how to take that information to continue to move forward and learn. It's important that we do so with intention. Remember, it's not about being right, it's about creating an environment in which students feel safe with you and with each other. We want to model the behaviors that we would like to see our students using when collaborating.

Making a mistake in front of my fourth graders is a teachable moment and it feels comfortable because we took the time to get to know one another and feel comfortable in our environment. However, the thought of making a mistake in front of a room full of educators or district employees who I do not know or have a rapport with makes me nervous. I'm talking heart racing, face reddening, sweaty upper lip *nervous*. Usually when I'm this nervous it is difficult to articulate my thoughts and I forget to breathe while I'm talking, which makes it even harder to share out. What I'm trying to say is, it's not easy to speak up in a room full of people you do not know or feel comfortable around regardless of age and we should realize that our students may have the same apprehension or anxiety in a new classroom.

I recently finished my administrative licensure classes with a cohort of fifteen other educators. I often think back to the first few classes in the program and how intimidated I was to share my thoughts with other educators in the room. I was even close friends with three of the women in my class, but that pesky, panicky feeling would overcome me every time I thought about sharing aloud. My professor, Dr. Scott McLeod, knew it was important that we get to know one another to share and collaborate in a meaningful way. We participated in at least three team building activities during each class for the first year.

As the first semester went on and team building activities were integrated into each class, I began to know my peers better. They became people with whom I felt comfortable and safe. By the fourth class I did not mind sharing out because I no longer feared being judged for my answers. I went from anxiety-ridden to excited about speaking up and sharing my ideas and hearing my peer's honest thoughts in return.

I felt safe and respected by my cohort peers which made me eager to share and collaborate. This is just one of many examples showing how creating a community among students in a classroom is fundamental to having a successful and collaborative classroom. We must ensure that we are setting aside time to guide relationship-building among our students through activities, modeling, and coaching to help them feel comfortable and safe around one another and develop the skills to work collaboratively.

"Classroom Community" is one of the more common buzzwords thrown around in the teaching world—especially on social media. You can type in #ClassroomCommunity into Twitter or Instagram and be immediately overwhelmed with posts about how teachers are building community among their students through community meetings, character words lessons, and STEM activities. It may be a buzzword, but having a strong and tightly woven classroom community holds true power. It is one of the most important foundational pillars for running a successful classroom where students feel safe to take risks and trust that they will not be judged by their teacher or peers. By taking the time throughout the entire year to continually work on building community and fostering positive relationships among students, we are providing an environment in which students feel safe to collaborate and learn.

When I look back on moments when I knew that the classroom community we had created encouraged students to take risks and make mistakes during the learning process, I think of one example that still stands out. It was during a math lesson led by one of my wonderful student teachers. I was sitting at my small group table with a few students helping them work through the first part of the math lesson. It was an exploratory number talk and students were encouraged to solve the given problem in any way they could. I love these exploratory problems because as an educator, you can highlight the many ways students solved the problem and how many different paths there are to producing a correct answer. It also highlights the different ways in which our brains work to understand a given problem.

As we were wrapping up the problem at my table, my student teacher chose a volunteer to go to the board to show how they had solved the problem. This student walked confidently to the board and began explaining how he had come to his solution. As he wrote an equation on the board, I realized he had made a slight mistake and the answer would be skewed because of it.

Our usual routine after sharing our answers or ideas in class is to use "talk moves" where students use hand signals to show if they agreed or disagreed with the answer to encourage active participation. The students are taught to participate during whole group lessons with hand signals in order to share a new idea, agree, disagree, or add onto what a peer has said. These hand signals encourage active participation from all students, not just the ones who are called on. As soon as the student finished his explanation, I could see multiple hands shaking in disagreement with his answer. I braced myself to jump in and help redirect the solution when the student took it upon himself to ask a peer why they disagreed with his answer. The classmate kindly pointed out his mistake and explained what the right answer should have been. Another student chimed in and let the student at the board know that they had made the same mistake and not to worry. Then, another student spoke up saying it was okay and that they all made mistakes. I looked to the student at the board to see tears welling up in his eyes. I was worried that he was upset at making a mistake in front of the class, but then he spoke up and said, "I love this class so much. I'm so glad to be a part of a class where it's okay to make mistakes. Thank you." He then went back to his spot and hugged a friend as he sat down. I was so moved by the entire interaction that I started to tear up. Before moving on with our lesson, I took a moment to let the class know how proud I was of their understanding, kindness, and empathy.

It is moments like this that solidify my belief that more learning can happen in a classroom when we make time to build up the connections and relationships among our students.

How Do You Get There?

Always remember that these important relationships do not happen overnight, and they need to be practiced and maintained throughout the entire school year. I take the first week or two at the beginning of the school year to immerse ourselves in get-to-know-you activities. These are not only for me to get to know the kids and vice versa, but also a way for them to get to know one another. Team building activities are huge when it comes to building relationships among students. It pulls them out of their comfort zones and slowly helps them become vulnerable with one another.

All students take to team building differently. Some are super pumped to partake and will jump right in. They may even showcase their leadership skills by taking charge of leading the group. These students can help you cheer on and motivate other students who may be apprehensive about participating.

Some students need some encouragement to partake. They do well with some extra words of inspiration from you and/or their teammates. They may begrudgingly participate, but once they start to feel more comfortable and realize that no one is going to poke fun at them, they will get into the activities a little more.

Then, there are some students who may act as if they're too cool for team building. These kiddos, I've learned, are usually the most self-conscious of messing up in front of others. Be sure to encourage them and point out what they're doing well and encourage them to show their technique or to share their ideas. By pointing out that it's already a good idea or technique, you've created a low-stakes environment for them to share and connect with their team.

Some quick tips for implementing successful team building in your classroom:

1. Put your students in teams of four or five and keep them in these same groups for at least a week of activities. You want them to build on the trust and momentum that they gain each day. If you switch up the teams, they would be starting each day from scratch.

2. If a student doesn't want to participate, do not make them. Let them watch or help you set up for the activity. Over time, they will see the fun in the activities and want to jump in. Forcing them to participate will make it harder for them to trust you or their team.

3. Encourage and promote collaborative behavior by giving specific feedback to students. Be wary of saying "I like/I love...". It is not our approval we want students to seek, but instead an intrinsic motivation to exhibit positive behavior. Example: Instead of saying, "I really liked how you cheered on your team," try: "The cheering you were doing for your teammates during their turn helped them feel supported! Great job!" This names the specific positive behavior in the student while keeping the focus on them rather than on your approval.

4. Try putting an emphasis on working together as a team, rather than winning. Is the point of this activity to win or lose or is it to practice working together? Think about rewarding extra points to teams who show patience, cheer one another on, and tell one another "Good job." Although an activity might have a winner at some point, teams can earn their way to the top through showing teamwork.

5. Take your students' needs into account and make sure your activities can be done by *all* your students. You want all your students to feel seen and be able to participate. There are

students who may feel left out in a lot of spaces due to limitations they may have, and you don't want them to associate that feeling with your classroom or with their classmates.

Let's walk through a few activities to build community among students:

Hula Hoop Challenge:
Grade Levels: 1-6
Materials: 1 Hula hoop for each team in your classroom
Prep:
  + Make sure the class is split up into teams of four or five students.
Directions:
  1. Give each team a hula hoop.
  2. Instruct them to stand in a line shoulder to shoulder and join hands. From this point on, the group cannot release their hands.
  3. The student at the end of the line needs to take the hula hoop and figure out a way to maneuver it across their body and pass it to the next student.
  4. The passing of the hoop keeps going until the student at the other end receives it and is able to maneuver it to their free hand.
  5. Once groups begin successfully passing the hoop across their team, join up two to three teams at a time to create a longer line and see if they can send all their hula hoops across the longer line of students.
  6. Work up to having the entire class create one long line (or circle at this point) and see if they can successfully pass all the hula hoops through the entire line of students without anyone releasing their hands.

During this activity I hear a lot of groaning when they hear they have to hold hands. Fourth grade is the year many students become acutely aware of themselves as individuals and holding hands is one of the last things they want to do. With some gentle encouragement, they usually start holding hands, but if a student is adamant that they do not want to hold hands, holding wrists works too. Soon though, they forget about the hand holding and you start to hear giggling and cheers when they figure out how to move the hula hoop from one end of their line to the other. What I like to listen for are students encouraging one another or coaching one another on how to move the hula hoop. I like to positively reinforce that behavior because that is what great teams do: encourage and communicate.

To switch it up, I've also had the teams time themselves and try to beat their best time. This activity is one of the first team building activities I do with my students because it's easy to explain, easy to do in the classroom, and it yields some great results in team bonding.

Rock, Paper, Scissors Champion:
Grade Levels: K-6
Materials: Just the students
Directions:
1. Have students pair up (teams won't matter for this activity).
2. In their pairs, they will compete in one round of rock, paper, scissors.
3. The winner of the round will continue to compete with students in the room while the other student becomes their personal cheering section.
4. The student who is still competing will walk around the room with their cheering section behind them cheering them on.
5. They walk around until they find another student still competing and they will compete in another round of rock, paper, scissors.

6. The winner of the rounds will continue to compete while the student who lost the round and all people cheering for them will join the cheering section of the winner.
7. This will continue until there are only two students left competing, each with their own cheering sections.
8. They will compete in one last championship round of rock, paper, scissors.
9. The winner becomes the Rock, Paper, Scissors champion and everyone cheers for them.

I've seen this played in professional developments and in classrooms kindergarten to sixth grade. In classrooms, I've seen it be very powerful when the teacher prefaced this activity with the *why* behind it. This activity isn't about winning and being a champion, but rather being happy for each other's successes. The best lesson that can be learned here is that we do not win all the time, but we can support our peers in their success. The emphasis should be on cheering rather than winning.

This activity is high energy and gets the students (and teachers) excited about cheering for one another. It moves quickly, so you can do a fair number of rounds in a ten-minute time period. Over the course of the year, I like to end random days with Rock, Paper, Scissors Champion. Since there is no prep and they know the rules, it is easy to start and complete as an activity five minutes before school lets out or even as an activity to start the morning. A great read aloud to read before playing any Rock, Paper, Scissor activities is *The Legend of Rock, Paper, Scissors* by Drew Daywalt.

Extreme Rock, Paper, Scissors:
Grade Levels: 2-6
Materials: 10-15 hula hoops OR chalk and a timer, outdoor space (preferably on concrete)

Prep:

- Line up all the hula hoops on the ground OR use chalk to draw 10-15 large circles one right after the other in a long line. It should look like this: OOOOOOOOOOOO
- Group teams together to create two large teams.

Directions:

1. Each team should line up behind the last hula hoop/circle on each end of the line.
2. The first player from each team should do a two-footed hop through as many hoops as they can until then come face-to-face (remind them to be mindful and not hop into each other).
   a. During this time, encourage students in line to be cheering on the teammate who is currently in play.
3. Once they meet in the hoops face-to-face, they must compete in a round of rock, paper, scissors.
4. The student who loses the round must step out of the line of hoops and rejoin their team's line while the winner of the round keeps hopping toward the opposing team's starting hoop.
5. Like a relay, the next student in line (from the team whose teammate lost the round) starts hopping to stop the oncoming student. Again, they will meet face-to-face in the hoops and stop to compete in a round of rock, paper, scissors.
6. The winner keeps hopping forward as many spaces as they can while the student who lost the round steps out. This repeats over and over again.
7. The object of the game is to reach the opposing team's starting hoop to win a point.
8. The team with the most points after five minutes wins.
9. You can play for as many rounds as desired.

Your students will beg to play this game again (so be prepared to play it a second time some time during the same week if you can). This game is another great opportunity to point out how to encourage our teammates from our lines. I like to see which line can cheer louder, with more excitement, or make the most original cheer. If you have a larger class size and lines are long, consider making two lines of hula hoops and having four teams instead of two in order to keep engagement high.

Extreme Tic-Tac-Toe:
Grade Levels: 3-6
Materials: 9 hula hoops OR chalk, 3 bean bags in 2 colors OR other items that can be used to be tic tac toe pieces
Prep:
- Set up your life-size tic-tac-toe board by arranging hula hoops in a 3x3 grid or drawing a life-size tic-tac-toe board on a concrete space outdoors.
- Group teams together to create two large teams.
- Split the bean bags or items of your choice by color.

Directions:
1. Have the two teams line up next to each other facing the tic-tac-toe grid.
2. This activity works like a relay race: The first three students in each line will have their team's colored bean bag in their hands.
3. When the teacher says "Go!" the first student in each line will run as fast as they can down to the tic-tac-toe grid.
4. They will then choose a space on which to place their tic-tac-toe piece. Once they choose, they will run back to their line and tag their teammate.
5. Once tagged, the next student in line will run down and place their piece in the grid and run back to their line.
6. The third teammate runs down and places their piece in the grid and runs back to their line.
7. The fourth player (and players following) will not have a tic-tac-toe piece, so they will run down to the grid and see if they

can move one of their team's pieces to get closer to making three in a row.

8. Teams will keep relaying and moving pieces on the board until one team gets three in a row.

Similar to *Extreme Rock, Paper, Scissors*, this game is high energy. It moves a bit quicker since it is a faster relay. I suggest playing one round first without having the team discuss strategy and see how it goes. For the second round, give each team some time to strategize how to best win their giant Tic Tac Toe game. After the second round I like to have them reflect as a team and compare the two rounds. Which round did they do better as a team? Why did they think they did better? What would they change if they played a third time? Again, if you have larger class sizes, consider making two Tic Tac Toe boards to make the relay lines shorter.

Clean Your Backyard:
Grade Levels: K-6
Materials: Sheets of paper for each student, masking tape **Can also be done with indoor reusable snowballs or soft gatorskin balls.
Prep:
   + Give each student a sheet of paper to crumble into a ball (these can be kept to reuse for future game play too.)
   + Group students together to create two large teams.
   + Place masking tape down the center of your room to split the room in half.
Directions:
1. With the room split in half, have one team stand on one side of the room and the other team stand on the remaining half.
2. Give all students a piece of paper to crumble into a ball.
3. Tell the students that they are trying to "clean their backyard" and clear all the paper balls off their side.

4. They have one minute to throw as many paper balls onto the opposing team's side.

5. The team with the least amount of paper balls on their side wins.

This game is about working as a team to complete a simple task. I've seen this done at day camps and in primary classrooms. Some teachers I've observed playing this have put a few more rules in place to encourage safety and lessen the chances of disagreements. In their version, students can only throw the paper balls underhand; they cannot throw them at a student (it's not dodgeball); they cannot kick the paper ball; and they cannot block the other team from throwing. Again, you can have them complete the first round without strategizing and then give the teams time to strategize for the second round. Finally, give them time to reflect on what they did well and what they would change for a third round.

Toothpaste Activity:
Grade Levels: 2-6
Materials: Tubes of toothpaste for each team (try the dollar store), paper plate for each team, access to a sink
Prep:
  + Have a tube of toothpaste and plate ready for each team.
Directions:
  1. Hand out the materials to each student team.
  2. Tell the teams that their job is to squeeze as much toothpaste out of the tube as possible. Make sure that all teammates have the opportunity to squeeze out some toothpaste.
  3. Once each group has squeezed all the toothpaste out ask: How easy was it to squeeze all the toothpaste out of the tube?
  4. Have students turn and reflect with their group, then have a couple groups share out.

5. Then ask: How can squeezing the toothpaste out of the tube relate to the way we talk to people or the actions we take?

6. Next, tell them to try and put the toothpaste back into the tube with only their hands—no tools!

7. As they are working, pose these questions for teams to think about:
   a. Was it easy to put the toothpaste back into the tube?
   b. Could you put *all* the toothpaste back into the tube?
   c. How does the toothpaste relate to our words and actions?

8. Have students wash their hands.

9. After all hands are washed, they can share out the responses they came up with to the questions posed during the activity.

This particular activity is one that I refer back to throughout the year and one that students remember for years after. They have a blast squeezing out all the toothpaste—you can hear the gleeful squeals as the activity starts. When you challenge them to put the toothpaste back into the tube, they work together to find the best way to maneuver the toothpaste back with their fingers. Over the years I have been impressed with the amount some students are able to get back into the tube. I had a team one year that filled most of the tube back up! However, the task is to put it *all* back in the tube and the fact that every single bit cannot be put back in is the whole point.

A coworker completed this activity in her second-grade classroom. She said it was a great hands-on and visual representation for the importance of reflecting on our words and actions and how they can affect others. She made sure to set specific expectations around what students were expected to do with the toothpaste and what they were not supposed to do with the toothpaste (like put it in their mouth!). Once a word or action is out in the world, it's difficult to completely take it back which is why we should be thoughtful of how we treat and speak to others.

Some follow-up questions to use would be: Think of a time when you said something you wished you could take back; how did you feel? Think of a time someone said something unkind to you; how did you feel? What strategies can we use to help us stop and think before we say something we cannot fully take back? Students can understand the impact of their words and actions as well as the repercussions of saying something that is unkind.

Complete the Puzzle
Grade Levels: K-2
Materials: Different printed pictures (nature scene, animals, school mascot, etc.) enough for each team on 8.5 x 11 paper, plastic baggies
Prep:
  + Cut the printed pictures into multiple pieces.
  + Place pieces of each picture into plastic baggies.
Directions
  1. Give each team a plastic baggie of puzzle pieces.
  2. Have each team work together to solve their puzzle.
  3. Once they finish, they should discuss how well they worked together.
  4. Repeat by switching the baggies around to different groups.

While talking with a friend who teaches second grade and completes this activity with her class each year, she explained that putting together a paper puzzle helped with both teamwork and executive functioning skills. There are times when she needed to help model what good teamwork looks like during the first puzzle, but by the third puzzle, teams would be working very well together.

Describe Yourself STEM Challenge
Grade Levels: K-6
Materials: Any type of building toys (LEGOS, Plus Plus Blocks, Brain Flakes, Hashtag Blocks, etc.), timer

Prep:

- ◆ Give each student access to building toys (a handful on their desk or a bucket on the table).

Directions:

1. Once students have their building materials, give them 5-7 minutes to build something that describes them.
2. After time is up, students share with their team or small group what their creation is and why it describes them.
3. Then, as a whole group, invite volunteers to share something they learned about a team member with the class.

I'm always amazed by the creations the kids come up with to describe themselves. One year I had a student make a box and person out of hashtag blocks for this activity. When he shared what he made with his teammates he said that he was an out-of-the-box thinker and that's why he created a person who represented him standing outside of a box. Not only do the students get to know each other better, but they also are able to take the time to think about who they are as individuals as well.

STEM Paper Chain Challenge
Grade Levels: 1-6
Materials: 8.5 x 11 in construction paper, masking tape, scissors, timer
Prep:

- ◆ Cut 1 ft of masking tape for each team.
- ◆ Make sure you have a piece of construction paper for each team.
- ◆ Make sure each team has a pair of scissors.

Directions:

1. Pass out the materials to each team.
2. Tell them they have five minutes to create the longest paper chain they can, using only the materials given to them.
3. Set a timer for five minutes and let them create!

4. When the timer goes off, have each team bring their chain to the front of the room to be compared.
5. The longest paper chain wins.

I really like doing this activity twice, so I always prepare double the materials in preparation for a second round. After the first final reveal, I have the teams reflect on their first round and think about what went well, what could be improved, and how they could change their strategy for the next round. Many times, I see groups that realized they had not conserved materials and ran out too soon or teams that needed to assign jobs to create an assembly line. It is inspiring to see students reflect on their progress and change their strategy based on what they saw other teams doing, how other chains were put together, or simply finding a better way to complete the activity. I once had a group go from having the shortest chain in the first round to having the longest chain by a foot and a half in the second round. The innovation and teamwork that goes into this activity allows students to be creative while also having to communicate and work together to find the best way to build the paper chain.

I have a friend who teaches first grade and completed this task with her first graders. She modeled how to make a paper chain and had her students practice first before making it a STEM challenge. After this modeling and practice, her first graders were ready to complete the challenge. I suggest increasing the time to seven or eight minutes for younger grade levels.

These activities are just the tip of the iceberg when it comes to team building and community building exercises that can be completed with students at the beginning of the year. If some of these activities don't work for your students—that is OK. Tweak them to fit the needs of your students or use completely different activities. The important thing to remember is to make time to allow your students to become comfortable with each other.

Flames in the Classroom #2:

Nicole Wong

Nicole is a sixth-grade teacher in Los Angeles, California. Here, Nicole shares an idea she uses to build community with her students at the beginning of the year:

What does it mean to build community among students? More importantly, how do we do it? For me, it all boils down to two words: relationships and trust. Effective teaching cannot happen without getting to truly know your students and showing them the value and impact of *their* voice in the classroom. A safe classroom community is built on the trust your students have for you and the trust your students have for each other. Building trust and making space for student voice and input cannot be done overnight...so where do we start?

A simple back-to-school activity I've launched both in person and virtually with my sixth graders is the popular ice breaker, *Two Truths and a Lie*. Pass out a notecard to each student and have them write their name, two truths, and a lie. Encourage your students to think outside of the box, to share three statements that no one knows about them, not even a close friend. Collect all the notecards into a basket. Every morning, pick a random notecard and engage the class in a discussion to guess which statement is the lie. Let that student author of that notecard have the spotlight, the stage, the attention. If implementing this activity virtually, create a Google Form asking students to fill out their name, two truths, and a lie. After their responses roll in, create a slide for each student displaying their two truths and a lie to share with students each morning.

The first time I played *Two Truths and a Lie* with my students, I did not expect the contagious laughter, the smiles, and the inside jokes that created the very first bonds of our classroom community. All it took was five minutes each morning, five minutes of focus on one special student, to let each student know that they matter. That their past experiences matter. That their hobbies, their quirks, and what they choose to share with us matters.

I've also built on this activity by turning it into a quiz game. Students are placed into small groups and asked to create a Kahoot with questions about each student. The questions can be true/false or multiple choice, covering virtually anything: fun and random facts. Each Friday, select a Kahoot to play with the whole class and watch as students begin to learn more about each other, and grow more comfortable with each other.

There is nothing more important than creating a classroom community that values, prioritizes, and makes space for student voice. In the eight years I've been teaching, I've learned that it's about the small goofy moments - the off topic, random conversations - that truly build community. It's these moments that humanize us beyond the roles of teacher and student, to human and human. Humans with stories, passions, and the desire to connect with other humans.

Connect with Nicole:
Instagram: @caffeinateandeducate
Teachers Pay Teachers: Caffeinate and Educate

Keep the Momentum Going with Community-Growing Activities

Activities like the ones listed above can be done at the beginning of the year as a great way to set the tone and your expectations around creating and maintaining a strong and safe classroom community. However, if these activities are where we stop, we miss the opportunity to build on the momentum created at the beginning of the year. Therefore, to ensure that the importance of community is instilled throughout the entire year, make sure that you have systems or activities to use over the course of the school year. Here are some ideas to continue building and strengthening classroom community throughout the year:

What Went Well:
Grade Level: K-6
Materials: None
Time: 3-7 minutes
Directions:
Implementing time for *What Went Well* in the morning is incredibly simple and easy to do:

1. When students settle in, as part of the morning routine ask students to share something that went well since you saw them last. This can be *anything* that a student found joy in.
2. Students who want to share, raise their hands.
3. Once a student shares, thank them for sharing and ask the class to give them two celebratory claps.
   a. I like claps because it gives a sense of acknowledgement to the student who shared and by limiting the number of claps, it keeps the routine moving in a timely manner.
4. Students can also share something that didn't go well if they feel comfortable.

    a. For students who share something that didn't go so well, I suggest doing one clap of solidarity and let them know you're holding space for them.

5. Any student who wants to share can share out at least once.

I love starting the mornings with *What Went Well*, because it starts us off on the right foot by celebrating the things that brought them joy. It also allows students to make connections with each other around their hobbies, traditions, sports, family dynamics, etc. Finally, it gives students a safe space to practice sharing out with the class, building their confidence so they can share out during academic discussions as well.

Spotted Wall:
Grade Level: 2-6
Materials: Sticky notes and wall space to place sticky notes
Prep: Create a small space in your classroom where students can place spotted notes acknowledging their peers.

+ Example: I have a small "Spotted" whiteboard with strings and clothes pins that has a character trait of the week attached to our classroom happenings wall. Students can fill out a Spotted Card and attach it to a clothespin to display.

Directions:
1. Create a small place in your classroom where students can acknowledge one other using what I like to call "Spotted Cards."
2. You can tie this acknowledgement to a character trait (if you do character trait lessons or curriculum) or you can leave it open ended for them.
3. Have sticky notes available near the Spotted Wall for students to write down the name of the student and what they want to acknowledge them for.

4. Then, they stick the finished spotted card or sticky note to the Spotted Wall.

5. Explain that you want students to "spot" each other for doing great things in the classroom and acknowledge them publicly for it.

6. Students can read the wall independently throughout the week and then take time at the end of the week to read out the Spotted Wall and give the Spotted Students the notes to keep that were written about them.

Having a place where students can lift up and acknowledge one another for the great things they are doing in the classroom has been a powerful way to let them know that they are being seen. Seeing their face light up when they've been "spotted" by a peer or when they say, "I didn't think anyone noticed that!" is one of the best scenes to watch play out in a classroom.

Community Sharing Space:
Materials: Online platform for sharing: Your School LMS (i.e. Google Classroom, Schoology, Canvas, etc.) or Padlet/Jamboard/Flipgrid.
Prep: Set up an album, folder, etc. where students have access to share from home.
Directions:

1. Set up your sharing platform (whichever way works best for your students).
2. Ask them to add photos or videos to the folder/album of things they are working on or enjoy at home (e. g., hobbies, sports, crafts, games, siblings, pets, etc.).
3. Take time during a morning or afternoon sometime during the week to publicly share out the items students have added to the folder.

As I write this book, I am teaching during the 2020-2021 COVID-19 pandemic. I've had to find different ways to get my students to connect and grow rapport with one another and this idea came about because students wanted to show each other all the things they were working on at home during virtual learning. We called it the *Saeedian Share Out.* Even when we went back to school in a hybrid capacity and then fully in-person, we kept this as a part of our routine and tradition on Friday mornings—because the kids *loved* being able to share what they were doing at home with each other.

Through this idea I had students collaborating on illustrations for a book they were co-authoring and sharing the designs with the class. I had students create videos about the rockets they were building from a set and how they worked, to students teaching how to make guacamole. I had students do tours of their "work areas" and the different crafts they were working on—which inspired other students to try that craft. The connection this folder created for my students was phenomenal and something I will continue to use for years to come.

Comment Cards:

Materials: Printed paper with student names on them, scissors

Prep: Create a Word document with student names on them. I suggest having two or four students per page. Cut the papers so that each student has an individual card.

Directions:

1. Pass out the individual comment cards at random to each student.

2. Ask that they write something positive about the student named on their card.

3. Next, you can choose one of two options:
   a. You can have the students give the cards directly to the student they wrote about.
   b. Students can turn the comment cards in to you and you can pass them out anonymously.

Comment cards were the brilliant idea of one of my students from my third year of teaching. She read about the idea in *Lemonade Wars* and thought it would be a great way to practice noticing positive attributes in her peers as well as filling someone's bucket. Anytime you can integrate student ideas—especially for the betterment of the community, it's a no brainer.

Community Meetings:

Materials: Community meeting protocol, sentence starters for that day, talking ball/stick

Prep:
   + Prep your sentence starters for the meeting.
   + Have your talking ball/stick available.

Directions:

Here is how I begin and manage my community meetings:

1. I run a community meeting once a week on Friday afternoons to allow students to reflect on the week and set goals for the next week.

2. I have a student of the week who runs my community meetings. It is a weekly job that is rotated through each one of my kids before the end of the school year—if you don't have a student of the week, you can schedule out the year for each student to run the meetings. I've found it is so much more powerful if the teacher takes a back seat and the students have the power to share and solve their own problems.

3. I run the community meeting for the first two weeks of school in order to model how it should look and sound. In the third week I have the students take over.

4. Once the meeting is handed over to the student of the week, they follow the community meeting protocol to help them run it—I am there for support, but otherwise I join the meeting like another student.

5. I pick out sentence stems beforehand and give it to the student of the week to present. I ask them to choose how they would like the class to greet each other. I choose a sentence stem that focuses on what I would like to reflect on for the week (e.g., reflecting on their work from the week, focusing on a character word, sharing about a family tradition, etc.).

6. I would suggest picking the handshake greeting and keeping it until all the students take it seriously and master it. Then I would move on to the more fun and silly greetings.

7. I also use a "talking ball." You can use anything like a beach ball, koosh ball, microphone, etc. to help manage side conversations.

   a. Create community meeting norms with students and read these at the start of each meeting. This can also be helpful in redirecting students with off task conversations.

8. Review the "Grievance Guidelines." It is incredibly important to follow the guidelines in order to keep the community meeting a safe space.

a. Grievance Guidelines:

    i.   Grievances are anonymous which means no names are to be used. Instead, use phrases like: "There is someone...", "There are people...", "I've noticed that..."

    ii.   Due to grievances being anonymous, if you realize a grievance is about your behavior—don't yell out (no one knows it's you, but you); listen and see how your actions are making others feel. Then, reflect on how you can make it better.

    iii.   Make sure the grievance you air is for the good of the group (something that can help better the class). If you're having a personal problem, it might be better to have a discussion with the teacher one on one.

    iv.   If you are sharing a solution, make sure your solution has not already been voiced and that you're sharing a strategy that is easily used and appropriate.

    v.   Remember, this is a tool to make our community even BETTER. Please be kind and thoughtful.

9. The first couple weeks I don't make students share unless they want to.

10. When students pass on sharing, I have a one-on-one conversation with that student later to try and see why they were nervous and how I can help (e.g., frontloading the topic they'll be sharing about, coming up with ideas to share together, or even a hand signal with me to show that they do or don't want to share so that I can navigate how to skip the student in the moment).

11. Even my most shy kiddos over the years have been able to open up and talk with encouragement and frontloading.

Community Meeting Protocol:

1. Ask everyone to join you at the community meeting area in a circle.

2. Introduce the greeting (Hello, _____. And shake hands or high five) and model it for everyone with a friend in the center of the circle.

3. Read the sentence stem for the week aloud. Tell your classmates that you will give them fifteen seconds to think about what they would like to share.

4. Ask, "Who would like to share first?" Choose one student to pass the speaking ball to—that student will pass it to the right or left of them to move around the circle.

5. Once everyone has shared, say," Thank you all for sharing. Now we will move on to grievances."

6. Ask if there are any grievances (issues or problems in the classroom students think need solving): "Is there anyone who would like to share a new grievance?"

7. Choose two students (one at a time) to share a grievance.

8. Once a grievance is shared, ask: "Does anyone have a solution to this problem?"

9. Choose two to three volunteers to share a solution for each grievance.

10. Share the second grievance and repeat the process with volunteers.

11. Say, "Thank you all for coming and that concludes the community meeting!"

12. You may conclude with applause or a class cheer.

I implemented weekly community meetings my second-year teaching and saw a huge difference between the community among students from my first year to my second. Putting twenty-five minutes aside each week to check in with one another and reflect can be a really powerful tool. My favorite way to reflect is to have students share something they felt went well that week and something that they want to work towards the next week. I have found that anonymous grievances help students advocate for things that they want to see change in the classroom. I also like that the students in the room are the ones coming up with solutions to the grievances. They learn how to advocate for themselves and find solutions to the problems they're facing in the classroom.

For example, one year I had a student mention that they were having a hard time walking in line because some students were giving their classmates "flat tires" (where the heel of the shoe is stepped on and the person's shoe pops off). When they shared how it made them feel I could see some of the students in the circle reflecting on their actions—in their eyes they saw flat tires as funny, but they had not realized that the students receiving the flat tires did not find it funny at all. After that meeting, the flat tires in line stopped. The power of community meetings and connecting with one another can be used throughout the school year to keep the community-building momentum going.

> Taking time at the beginning of each year to help students get to know each other and practice collaboration skills pays dividends throughout the school year.

Taking time at the beginning of each year to help students get to know each other and practice collaboration skills pays dividends throughout the school year. Creating an environment in which everyone feels safe to take chances and try something new enables your classroom to become a place where students can truly learn from their mistakes. If we tell them mistakes are proof they're trying, the educators in the room need to create a space where those mistakes will not be judged because it is not necessarily the mistake that is scary, but rather making the mistake in front of others. By building a strong and caring classroom community you can decrease the fear students feel about making mistakes in front of others and increase their capacity to learn together in a safe space.

Be the Flame Actions

Reflect on your classroom community from past years, and consider the following:

- Hold a community meeting for your students to share and reflect together.
- Use comment cards this week to give your students the opportunity to spread positivity.
- Ask your students to share something that went well one morning this week.

CHAPTER 4

Stoke

Teachers must *Stoke* the momentum of the community they've started in the classroom and use it to create a community of collaboration.

"A team is not a group of people who work together. A team is a group of people who trust each other."
                    – Simon Sinek

Building a Community of Collaboration

When I started teaching my first year and even into my second and third years, I didn't quite understand the power of collaboration among students. I had never truly seen It modeled in the classroom. Growing up, I had always completed classwork by myself. The classrooms that I spent time in while receiving my teaching license had students working independently. Group projects occurred in both situations, but they were never the norm. I can remember how excited we would get when a teacher would announce that the project we were starting was a group project. Cheers would go up around the room until the teacher announced that she would be choosing our groups. The excitement, although still there, would be dampened as we all realized we wouldn't be placed in groups with our friends.

I brought this dated idea that students had to work alone with me into my first couple years of teaching. If I let students collaborate wouldn't that be considered cheating? How could I tell what an individual student knew if a group of students had done the work together? What if they were off task? I felt that all activities needed to be done independently so I knew how well students understood the material, I knew they weren't cheating, and I could easily see if someone was off task. I would walk the classroom, helping students who looked stuck. If you had glanced into my classroom, you might have seen what looked like engagement in their work and every student *must* understand the material if they were working, right? Wrong. I was struggling to help each student who didn't understand and felt like I was being pulled in ten different directions.

I had a student my third year who wanted to be a teacher when she grew up. She was 10 years old going on 30—I swear, she may have been more mature than I was! I noticed that whenever I was busy helping a student and another student raised their hand for help, she would walk over, give them some guided help, and then walk back to her desk. It hit me then: Why am I not using the knowledge and know-how of students in our classroom to support one another? It seemed ridiculous that it had taken me this long to realize that I should not have to do it all on my own. It truly takes a village, and I should be using our village to provide support from within.

Education in America can be incredibly individualistic. There is little emphasis on the success of the group, but rather emphasis on the success of individuals. What if we started to push back against this outdated status quo and helped students learn to support one another as a collective?

Flames in the Classroom #3

Derrick Carlson

Derrick is a second-grade teacher in Chicago, Illinois. Here, Derrick shares different ways to encourage collaboration and discussion in the classroom:

Collaboration and investment are vital for students working together and they help cultivate a classroom's collective success. Protection of all voices, ownership of the shared physical space, and whole group discourse that elevates student contributions is part of the path to collective success in a collaborative classroom. Empowering students and giving them shared ownership while elevating how we must invest in each other facilitates a collaborative and just classroom. Author Zaretta Hammond teaches us that raising oxytocin is a key factor in creating a space that is socially and emotionally safe for students, which will lead them to taking academic risks if they feel their thoughts and contributions will be validated and protected. Engagement improves when students publicly hear how their contribution is adding to the discussion. Other students see and value each other's work and are more likely to respect and work with the other student. This takes practice and it is a life skill in and beyond the classroom that helps to build bridges and connect others for collaborative work.

Classroom jobs and shared investment in the physical space is important to the success of the collective collaboration. The collaborative investment and management of the classroom space by students sends the message that we all invest in the classroom space together and everyone matters. Partners working on a task together and a routine where they can give each other authentic praise, and eventually constructive feedback, reinforces that interest in investing with one another.

To get students to invest in and develop a desire to collaborate with each other, it is important as the educator to find a space and time to elevate how each individual contribution can connect to the lesson. I personally like to think of the conversation as a web, instead of a linear model that has a beginning that leads to an end goal. Framing our conversations as linear with simply a goal in mind can incidentally lead to a fast-achievement mentality and reinforces outcome and output-oriented thinking and talk patterns. This "get to the goal" mentality does not engage the student to think critically, engage with information or process how new information connects to prior knowledge that can be used to innovate and create. If the focus is mastery as quickly as possible, the classroom academically can become about completion for the sake of compliance. This elevates those who can do a task quickly and diminishes the contributions of others who may be really creative and need more time to process information. Students need to make relevant connections and the whole group conversation can elevate how each voice is important for collaboration and enriching the discourse.

Academically, our discourse should reflect ways students can make meaningful connections between what is being said and information with which they may come in contact. This can look like a teacher making a connection between a child's story about sharing items at a birthday celebration and discussing even and odd numbers. The abstract becomes relevant, and the other students witness the teacher making the story connect to the lesson. Other examples could be relating travel stories to geology, climate, and weather topics. Making the work interdisciplinary and the academic conversations reflect interdisciplinary and integral work will elevate the power of the interconnection skill. This builds their interest in collaborating with each other instead of finding like-minded reinforcement, which stagnates innovation.

While it is important to be clear with the objectives of a lesson, putting on blinders to disregard or only elevate specific contributions only invalidates their voice, which diminishes student interest in collaboration. For students who have been historically marginalized, this potentially reinforces the negative messages of society. If a student provides an off-topic piece of information, ask them kindly to try to make the connection or provide the reason why they added that piece of information. Follow up with a reinforcing acknowledgement that honors their voice. You have put the power in their space and you are the facilitator of their learning, collaboration, and practicing a conversational skill. Student sharing can be information for what that student needs and for us to be responsive to creating a classroom space that protects the collective and encourages collaborating with others of various backgrounds.

Connect with Derrick:
Instagram: @blackandbrightin2nd

How Do You Build a Community of Collaboration?

Building a community of collaboration starts with team building activities that you do at the beginning of the year that were discussed in Chapter 3. These activities will help you to ignite members of your team, community, family, collective, etc. It's here that you start to emphasize the importance of not leaving a team member behind, including everyone cheering one another on, helping one another out, and coaching how to work together and not next to one another. You'll hear me refer to the phrase, "working together, not next to one another," often, as it is important that the emphasis around group work stays focused on students *collaborating* about the work, not simply working as individuals in a group setting. Coaching students and teaching them the skills to work together is imperative to the success of meaningful collaborative work. If students are not provided the tools and skills to work collaboratively, they end up working as individuals. This can lead to resentment from students who are engaging in the work while other students copy it down, and the lack of engagement leads to lower academic outcomes as a whole.

During the rollout of collaborative work one year, I was watching a group that seemed to show more and more dissonance the longer they worked together. I could tell that one student had taken a leadership position and was calmly trying to engage another student in working together. However, that student had no desire to work with the group. They ignored the pleas of their team members and worked ahead of the group for the entire math block. I wanted to wait and see how the group handled the situation before stepping in. I could tell that the student who was trying to pull the group together was frustrated, so I pulled him into the hallway to talk about what was going on. The student explained that the other group member refused to work with them no matter how hard he attempted to include them in their conversation. Then, the student burst into tears and said, "Teachers always group me with the 'bad' kids in class because they think I can help them. I try my best to help them and I know teachers think I'll rub off on them, but it's hard." Wow. I realized there was a lot to unpack here.

First, we discussed that there are no "bad" kids, but there are students who might need a little more support and they ask for that support in different ways. Secondly, I reassured him that it is not his job to teach anyone how to collaborate. In fact, that's *my* job. I promised that I would spend time during the math block with their group to model collaborative behavior, coach them through tough discussions, and monitor the progress of that group's collaboration. Finally, I apologized for making him feel that he was given the responsibility of changing the behavior of another student—again, that was not his job; his job was to learn. This story shows the importance of making time at the beginning of the year to coach and model positive collaboration and not simply put it on students to manage and figure out.

Naming Collaborative Behaviors

I like to start the year by explicitly naming and modeling collaborative behavior. By explicitly naming collaborative behavior and modeling what it looks like, you are giving students a specific example for meeting collaboration norms. Once you name and explicitly model a behavior you can refer back to it by name and ask students to assess if they are meeting expectations.·

Terms that I use and how I introduce them:

Active Participation: Fully engaging in the work with team members by discussing what they believe the steps are to complete an assignment and checking in with one another on their understanding and feedback of how fast or slow they are moving.

1. I model this by having a couple of volunteers pretend to be my group members as we work together to solve a math problem (usually something simple that they would have mastered the year before).
2. I like to have us sit in the front of the room in a tight group with our notebooks on our laps facing each other.
3. I begin by checking to make sure everyone is ready to work.
4. I ask what they think we should do first and wait for someone to volunteer a starting point.

5. Once a starting point has been stated, I ask the other group member if they agree with that starting point.

6. Once we all agree, we solve the first step together and I check to see if we all found the same answer.

7. I then ask what we should do next and wait for a group member to voice what they think.

8. We begin to solve and suddenly I stop, saying: "I don't quite understand how you got that answer," and ask, "Could you show me how you completed that step?" Then, one of the students walks through how to solve that step. I thank them and we move on.

9. Once we all understand again, we continue to finish solving the problem.

10. Repeat steps 4-6 until the problem is solved.

Active participation by all group members is critical to the success of the group. The goal is to move forward together, not separately. If a student doesn't understand why a step is being done, then the group slows down to explain. With active participation, all members are checking for their understanding and advocating for help when needed. Again, team building at the beginning of the year is crucial to fostering an environment in which students can ask for help and receive positive feedback from their peers.

Passive Participation: Sitting back and not helping, doing something unrelated to the group work at hand, and allowing the group to do the work for you.

1. I model this by, again, having a couple of volunteers pretend to be my group members as we work together to solve a math problem (I usually use the same volunteers and have them work through the problem we just did).

2. Again, I have us sit in the front of the room in a tight group with our notebooks on our laps facing each other.

3. This time, I ask another group member to start the problem and to keep working through the problem together.

4. I start doodling on my notebook as the other group members solve the problem, then I gaze off into space, and I try to talk to another student who is not in our group.

5. Then, when the group has finished, I'll ask, "What did you all come up with?" and hurriedly copy down the answer.

Now, students will think the modeling of passive participation is hilarious—it's not very often that they see their teacher showing such off-task behavior. To bring it back to seriousness, I ask a couple of reflection questions for students to turn and talk about and then share: How do you think the other group members felt when I didn't help solve the problem? How do you think they felt when I just copied down the answer? If I didn't help solve the problem, how well do they think I understood the skill? This will help ground your point that passive participation is not only harmful to the students in the group doing the work without help, it's also harmful to the person who is passively participating because they aren't practicing their own skills.

Active Listening: Listening to what someone else is saying and being able to add onto, agree with, or disagree with what they were saying.

1. I usually practice this with the entire class as a whole because active listening isn't just for group work, it's important to use during mini lessons, too.

2. I tell them it's incredibly important that they listen to everything I am saying to be able to repeat it back to me or respond if they agree, disagree, or want to add to what I am saying.

3. Then I say something outrageous like, "I absolutely love giving homework. I think I should give even more homework!"
4. I ask students to then raise their hands to respond to my remarks and I promise you will have a lot of spirited responses from your students.

It's important that we teach active listening as a collaboration skill as well as a learning skill. It's the type of listening we want to encourage during lessons so that students are engaged and can have meaningful conversations during lessons as well as in their groups about what they're learning.

Passive Listening: Knowing that someone is speaking, but not knowing what they said.

1. This one is simple to model; I tell students to listen to what I'm about to say.
2. Then I proceed to say, "blah, blah, blahah, blah-blah."
3. Then I ask students to respond to what I said.
4. They're usually very confused at this point, so I ask a question instead: Could you tell that I was talking? Yes. Could you tell me what I said? No.
5. That's passive listening, you *know* I'm talking, but have not processed what I am saying. That is why it's so important that we focus our brains on the speaker and practice active listening.

By naming passive listening and giving an example of what it feels like, we are able to help students self-monitor their own listening behaviors. I will stop during lessons and ask, "I want you to self-assess: Are you actively listening or passively listening?" Pause to have them assess themselves. Then I follow up with, "How is your listening impacting your learning?" Pause to let them self-assess. This is not a time when you ask them to share out or show their assessment in any way, but rather provide them the opportunity to check-in with themselves metacognitively.

The "Bossy Tone": The name for the tone used with attitude, snark, or disrespect. NOTE: this tone is different from a student's normal or natural speaking voice or dialect. We should not be tone policing based on natural dialect, phrasing, or cultural background. Please be mindful of this.

I introduce the *"Bossy Tone"* to help my students understand what it sounds like to collaborate respectfully with one another and what it sounds like when they are not being respectful to one another. Usually, I hear the "Bossy Tone" come out when a student is feeling frustrated.

1. I explain that *how* we use our words is just as important as the words we use.
2. The "how" is the tone we use when talking. A sentence can sound very different depending on the tone we use.
3. I then model how this sounds using the exact same sentence twice: once with a calm tone and once with the *"Bossy Tone"* tone.
   a. Calm tone: "Hey, you're sitting in my seat."
   b. *Bossy Tone:* "Hey! You're sitting in my seat!"
4. I ask which way would they prefer to be talked to: Tone 1 or Tone 2?
5. Then, I give Tone 2 a name: the Bossy Tone
6. I explain that with the second tone, it sounds as if I'm bossing someone around.
7. I then say that the Bossy Tone has no place in our community because our main goal is to make everyone feel included and respected.
8. I also tell them that from now on I'll be listening for the Bossy Tone. I front load the students explaining that if I hear the tone,

that I'll point out the tone to them and ask them to try using their words again without the tone—they're not in trouble at all, we're just practicing using our words kindly.

Two *very* important things to remember when pointing out the tone when students are using it: First, this is not meant to be a "gotcha!" moment. We are not trying to catch our students doing something wrong or getting them in trouble, but rather partnering with them to help them communicate effectively. Second, when you point out the tone to a student, it must be communicated calmly and with empathy. If a student is feeling extremely frustrated, suggest taking some deep breaths or taking a break to regulate themselves so they can come back and communicate effectively with their group.

What I've found over the years is that students sometimes don't realize that they've slipped into using the tone because it's become a habit. I used this tone as a kid and hadn't ever realized it until one very memorable afternoon. When I was ten years old, I was in the car with my father and I could not, for the life of me, remember what he said, but I remember that I replied with a Bossy Tone, "What-ever." He then proceeded to tell me not to talk to him or anyone like that and being the pesky ten-year-old that I was, I responded with another Bossy Tone, "Sor-ry," which I hadn't meant to say using the tone, but it just came out.

We had just turned into our neighborhood and my father promptly pulled over and told me to get out of the car and walk the rest of the way home to give me time to think about how I talk to people. Let's just say that I didn't use that tone again. I like sharing that story with my students to show that I, too, had to practice and be reminded to make sure that I was using my words kindly.

I've found over the years that giving this tone a name makes it easy to identify and less ambiguous to students. This explicit explanation and modeling has been very powerful in my classroom because students can better communicate with each other and even advocate for themselves when they feel another student is using a Bossy Tone with them.

After introducing the terms, make sure to use them often and use them when stating your expectations for the group work time. I always state my expectations at the top of each lesson or at the top of work time. It might sound like, "My expectations are that all group members are actively participating and actively listening to one another while completing your assignment. Remember to work with each other, not next to one another." This sets the stage for what you will be looking for as you hop from group to group. If I see a student off task, I might quietly ask them if they are actively or passively participating with their group. Once they've self-identified, I ask them: How can you become an active participant? Rather than just reminding them to stay on task, help them decide how they can be a more active group member.

Now that students have the verbiage and explicit examples of important collaborative behaviors, you can begin coaching and modeling how to actively collaborate within a group.

Coaching Collaboration

Remember that phrase I said I would come back to throughout the chapter? Here it is again: work *with* one another, not *next to* one another. We want to encourage students to work collectively rather than as individuals because they can learn more by discussing the material and learning from each other rather than processing the information by themselves. Students possess a plethora of information and understanding. A student in your classroom could potentially explain a concept to another student in a different way that helps them grasp the material in a way they hadn't before. That is why it is so important to foster collaborative groups in the classroom. They can act as a built-in support structure, increase student-engagement, and therefore potentially increase learning outcomes.

So how do you shift the culture of working next to one another to working with each other? I do it through monitoring groups and noticing certain behaviors to determine who may need more support. You can spot groups that are working next to each other rather than with each other by seeing where they are in their work. If all the students are on different problems or at different parts of the assignment, it is obvious that they're not collaborating on the same problems together. Groups that are truly working together will be in lockstep through their entire assignment.

I use the M.A.T.H. workshop model for my math block. The acronym stands for **M**eet with the Teacher, **A**t Seat Work, **T**echnology, and **H**ands On Activity. During "At Seat Work" time, students work in collaborative groups to problem solve together. I create these groups using data from pretests taken before each unit. Each group is made up of three students: one student who needs little to no support, one student who may need some support, and a student who will need more support. Each group is a triad and able to help one another work through their assignment. This built-in support frees me up to pull small groups of students from other stations to reteach or enrich.

During the roll out of M.A.T.H. workshop one year I noticed that one group of students was not quite working with each other as we had been practicing for weeks by this point. I did a "walk around" during which I widely circle a group to watch and listen to how they work together. I saw that two students were working collaboratively through a math problem but becoming stuck throughout the problem. Meanwhile, the third student was four problems ahead of their group members and working independently.

I sat down with the group and asked how it was going. The two students working together said that they were doing okay. However, they were a little confused and their third group member would not help them. I turned to the third group member and asked why she was so far ahead and she replied, "Because I want to finish my work first. Then, I'll help them." I realized that her idea of helping their group was to get all the answers first and then help. I followed up with a question: Are you working *with* your group or *next to* your group? She thought about that and said, "Next to." I pointed out that even if they finish the work, it's not about individual completion, it's about group completion.

I asked the group members working together to explain how it felt to have to work without their third group member. They said that they felt a little hurt, excluded, and frustrated because all they wanted was to work together. I acknowledged that the third student wanted to help but asked her to reflect on whether letting the group struggle without her was more helpful than simply working together in the first place. The student sat for some time and then said, "I guess it would have been better to work together." The group members agreed, and I asked if they could try working together starting on a brand-new problem. They agreed and got to work.

This is just one example of many conversations I've had with students about working together in groups. Our education system emphasizes individual success rather than group success and it shows with the skill set students—especially younger students—have when it comes to working with others: Me first, then us. We need to reframe this approach so that it is simply: Us first.

Rolling out collaborative group work at the beginning of the year (or whenever you decide to start) takes time and care. As I've said before, not all students come into the classroom with a strong skill set for group work and it is our job to act as coaches and cheerleaders during this time. We are there to give meaningful feedback and celebrate their collective successes. If we spend the time up front in coaching collaboration, it pays dividends throughout the year as groups start to work like a collective.

Explicit Modeling

When I start coaching students to collaborate, I usually observe each group for a few minutes. If I notice that a group is having a difficult time working as a collective and are working more as individuals in a group setting, that is when I will ask to be a part of their group. When I become a part of their group, I let them know that I'm going to take more of a leadership role in their group to help model how the conversation should sound while working through a problem together. Here is a mock script of how that modeling would sound like:

Teacher: All right, so the problem says that Jack had 45 baseball cards, Juan had 30 baseball cards, and Chris had 25 baseball cards. How many baseball cards do they have all together? Katie, what do you think we need to do to solve this problem?

Katie: I think that because it says "all together" that we may need to multiply.

Teacher: Interesting thought; Darius, what do you think?

Darius: I actually think we need to add because it asks how many cards do they all have together.

Katie: Oh, that makes sense. I agree with Darius.

Teacher: All right, Cameron, what do you think? Do you agree that we need to add or disagree?

Cameron: I agree with Darius and Katie; I think we should add.

Teacher: Great! How should we go about adding these numbers together? Anyone have any ideas?

Cameron: I think we should add 45 and 30 first and then add 25 to the answer.

Darius: I agree.

Katie: Same.

Teacher: Ok, so let's add and check in with each other on our work.

After I model working through a question with a team, I'll ask them what they noticed about how I led the conversation. Usually, they'll say things like, "Everyone talked" or "We all had to agree before solving the problem" or "We talked about the way we could solve the problem." I'd acknowledge and praise them for what they noticed and agree that those are all ways that you worked *with* each other. We must communicate and agree. If we don't agree, there must be a dialogue about it so that you can either decide on one thing or compromise. Then, I ask if one of the students wants to take my role in leading the discussion. I'll sit and listen to that student move through the problem and I'm there to help prompt or remind as necessary. Then, I ask if another student could lead the discussion and so on.

This may seem a bit rigid and structured, but the structure helps students practice checking in with each other throughout the problem or assignment. As the year progresses and students get the hang of collaborating, the structure relaxes a bit into more of a conversation.

Using Sentence Stems to Structure Discussion

Sometimes finding the words to have an unstructured collaborative conversation about an assignment or problem can be difficult. Having sentence stems readily available for students to use in their conversations as they are getting acclimated to these discussions can be very helpful. You can create an anchor chart with them and post it in the room, write them on the board, or have them on a student handout. Here are some examples of sentence stems to use:

+ What do you think?
+ Where should we start?
+ Do you agree or disagree?
+ I agree because _____.

+ I disagree because _____.
+ I don't understand; can you explain?

These are incredibly simple, but they provide a little more structure and scaffolding to a discussion, giving students somewhere to start. I like to begin with the sentence stems in my classroom when we first start collaborating and phase them out as students become more comfortable with engaging in these conversations on their own.

Use of Discussion Protocols

While collaborating as a whole group, using protocols help structure these conversations so that students know exactly what to expect and can participate accordingly. When we take away the unknown, students are more likely to want to participate because it's low risk.

Talk Moves - I use talk moves in my classroom both in whole group and small group collaboration. It's a great visual way for students to show they're actively listening to the discussion and helps students facilitate their own conversations without my help.

I usually facilitate a few discussions in class, but once students are showing that they have the hang of it, I allow them to move into facilitating the discussion themselves. This usually looks like me picking the first person to speak, but then the speaker chooses who speaks after them and so on. The more ownership of the discussion that I can hand over to students, the better.

The talk moves are hand signals paired with a sentence stem. This sentence stem, again, helps structure the conversation and allows students to focus on sharing their ideas rather than how they're going to introduce their ideas. Once we start using them, they become second nature to students and they will start using them on their own, even without the structure of a class discussion.

Here are the talk moves I use in my classroom:

+ One Finger Up: *New Idea*
+ Sentence Stem: I think that _____.
+ Two Fingers Up: *Add-On*
+ Sentence Stem: I want to add onto what _____ said. I think that _____.
+ Shaking Thumb: *Agree*
+ Sentence Stem: I agree with _____ because _____.
+ Shaking Entire Hand: *Disagree*
+ Sentence Stem: I disagree with _____ because _____.
+ Thumb and Pinky Shake (sort of like "hang loose"): *"Me, too."*
+ I allow students to use this sign when they agree with the speaker or had a similar idea they were going to share, but don't want to

add to the discussion. This allows students to still participate in the discussion, without the pressure of being called on.

Collaborative Groups to Whole Group Discussion - Similar to a think-pair-share, when we have class discussions, I pose a question to the group and have them think independently about it. Then, I give them time to discuss in their collaborative groups to check-in and hear what other students think. I find that doing small collaborative discussions first with teams that they work with each day and feel comfortable with is helpful because they can have honest conversations about the questions before sharing out in front of the entire class. Once the teams have had time to discuss, I open the question up for whole-group discussion where students use their talk moves to share their thoughts with the whole class.

When Collaboration is Hard

Collaboration is a beautiful tool and an important skill for all students to learn; however, some students may need more support in growing their skills to be thoughtful collaborators with a group. You may have students in your room who have a harder time collaborating and it's important to take their needs into account. Try these ideas for students who need more support to become successful collaborators:

1. Front load the student by discussing expected collaboration behaviors and unexpected collaboration behaviors.
2. Discuss which times of the day they feel confident in collaborating and then give them the choice to work independently during other times throughout the day.
3. Set collaboration goals with the student. Discuss what reaching the goal will look like and a reward for achieving that goal. Make sure to ask the student to help you come up with reward ideas so they're motivated to reach it.

4. Give the student a role in their group to focus on, such as a timekeeper (keeps track of the time left in group work), summarizer (summarizes what was said when discussing each problem), or task manager (ensuring that all students are on task and working with the group).

These are some ideas I've used in the past with students who have had emotional needs, were neurodivergent, or just needed some extra support. Collaboration is an important, but difficult, skill to master. Building up stamina can help students work towards collaborating with their peers more effectively and more often. Make sure not to push students who need more support into a collaborative situation in which they feel uncomfortable. It's important to partner with the student in order to build a foundation of trust and cultivate an environment in which they feel safe.

By meaningfully using collaborative groups and promoting collective success, we are helping our students to build social-emotional skills as well as academic skills. Group work helps students become proactive rather than reactive. They learn to problem solve and they learn to compromise. They learn to actively listen to each other and find ways to actively participate, giving feedback, assigning jobs, etc. These are skills that must be explicitly taught *and* practiced. Creating positive teacher-student relationships as well as positive relationships among students is a must in order to have a strong and effective classroom culture focused on high levels of learning for all.

> By meaningfully using collaborative groups and promoting collective success, we are helping our students to build social-emotional skills as well as academic skills.

Be the Flame Actions

Reflect on the following questions relating to collaboration in your classroom and then consider the following:

+ How often do you have students collaborate?
+ When students collaborate, do they work *with* each other or merely *next to* each other?
+ Do you stay away from group work because it creates conflict?
+ Pick a lesson for students to work in collaborative groups to have them practice working *with* each other.
+ Hold a class discussion and implement talk moves to encourage active listening and participation.
+ Label and model collaborative behaviors in your classroom to enhance student understanding around how to work with a group.

CHAPTER 5

Catch

Teachers must work to make the relationships they're building in the classroom *Catch* on with families, too. It takes a village, and communication and connection are powerful tools.

"Individually we are one drop. Together, we are an ocean."
– Ryunosuke Satoro

Building Community with Families

If you were to ask me during my first-year teaching what scared me the most about starting my new profession, I would have told you, "Parent phone calls." I started my teaching career incredibly fearful of building relationships with families. I had it in my head that contacting parents happened only when something negative occurred. However, I came to realize that is not the case at all. In fact, those negative interactions should be the exception, not the rule, when it comes to contacting families of the students we teach. As teachers, we have the opportunity to initiate more positive interactions with families than negative. These positive interactions build the foundation to help students feel supported and become successful in the classroom. Having these foundational relationships in place can also make those difficult phone calls a lot easier because both students and their families will know that you have the best intentions for their child.

One year I had a student who was having a hard time transitioning back into the school year after summer break. I tried so many things in the classroom to help ease them into our new routines, but they all fell flat. This was the year that I was moved out to a portable classroom and started flexible seating in that space. In addition to transitioning back into a school routine, students were also learning the new rules for being in a portable classroom and using an entirely new protocol for classroom seating. After a few weeks, this particular student and I felt exhausted and frustrated. I finally reached out to his family to see if they had any ideas.

After talking with the student's mom, it broke my heart to find out that the child was going home each day asking to switch schools. He was so defeated by what wasn't working, that he wanted to go to an entirely different school. I reassured the mother that all I wanted was for her son to feel comfortable and confident in our classroom. I asked if there was anything that they did at home that helped him transition into new situations that I could use in the classroom to create an environment that was familiar. I wanted to let her know that we were a team in supporting her child and in doing so, we created the foundation for a strong relationship that would last throughout the year.

That one phone call created a partnership between us, a partnership in which we were both working to support this child. Together, we decided that choosing an assigned seat together would be helpful for routine, we integrated more snack times throughout the school day which helped keep energy and focus high, and we both held high academic expectations for the student while also letting him know that we cared for him. After a few weeks of open communication and consistency in expectations from home to school, this student settled in and no longer wanted to switch schools! We had a fantastic year together, but I could not have done it without the support of the child's family. In fact, I received an email from this mom years later thanking me for working with her child because he was able to thrive upon entering middle school. Having the help of his family was the reason we were able to have such a successful year.

How Do You Go about Creating Relationships with Families?

There are a few small things that go a long way in creating relationships with families. You want the families to know that you are both on the same side when it comes to supporting their children. It's important for families to know that we want their child to succeed and grow as much as possible. They should know that we believe in their children and want to partner with them to make learning an enjoyable experience.

> The backbone of building rapport with families is communicating with families.

Communication with Families - The backbone of building rapport with families is communicating with families. It's important that you have a few things in place to make communicating with families successful. Here are a few ideas to put into action so that families feel connected to you while also maintaining some important boundaries:

Use the communication methods that your families prefer

Depending on your school's communication protocols, you may have some flexibility in how you communicate with your families. In the past, I've had complete reign over how I choose to connect with families and other years we've had one communication platform used on a school-wide basis. If you have the freedom to choose, I suggest reaching out to families with a survey, either paper-based or with a Google Form to see what their preferences are. There may be some families that do not have consistent access to technology and communicating with them via paper or phone would be easier, while some families may prefer an app through which they can get updates sent directly to their phones via text, while still others may prefer email.

It's important to get feedback from families because they are the ones with whom you are trying to connect. Having insight into the best communication method for them allows you to better get in touch with families for important information, discussing students' needs, and newsletters. Based on that feedback you can decide what is the best way to communicate with your families.

Another piece of information that is important to ask families is their preferred communication language. If you have families that speak a language other than English at home and they feel more comfortable communicating in their native language, there are school-communication apps that can translate into a variety of languages. Although it may not be perfect, it is one step closer to lessening the language barrier and allowing families to feel connected to you and the school.

Use a consistent platform of communication

Commit to using a consistent platform for your family-based communication. You can also choose to connect primarily via an app, email, or paper newsletter. This makes it easier on you and your families to know where to look for communication rather than having to look in two or three different places for questions and updates.

I choose a platform (again, try to base it off family feedback if you can) and send the platform information to parents via email before our

Meet and Greet night. This is prior to school starting and gives them time to set up an app if needed. This also gives them time to reach out for support if they need it as well. I find that frontloading families with information on how to set up new apps helps a lot. A PDF or screen-cast with step-by-step instructions for how to get started goes a long way. You'll be fielding less questions by frontloading families with this information, which is less stressful for both you and them.

Currently, there are many different platforms from which to choose when connecting with your families. *Remind* is specifically a communication app (with translation capabilities), *Seesaw* is a student portfolio app with communication abilities (with translation capabilities), *Class DoJo* is a classroom management app with communication abilities (with translation capabilities). While these are some apps I have used, there are many other options as well. I suggest checking with your administration or district technology team to see if there are apps that are not supported due to privacy issues. Remember, as the teacher, you must ensure that the platform you choose protects the privacy of your students and families.

In the past, I've used *Remind* and *Seesaw* regularly. With *Remind*, families subscribed to my *Remind* account through a text message and I can send out information blasts that are delivered to families as text messages. They can respond directly to me via the text message, if needed, and it comes directly to my *Remind* app. This was a great way for parents to connect with me if they had a quick question or needed to get in touch with me throughout the day.

Recently, my school moved to having a consistent, school-wide platform for communication. The app chosen by the staff was *Seesaw Learning*. I like using *Seesaw* because I can communicate with families and students can communicate with them, too, by sending home videos and pictures of their work in class. Families download the app and can communicate with me via direct message and communicate with their children by liking and commenting on their work. Seesaw has been a great way to connect with families and show them what is happening in the classroom.

Have a routine for your communication

This idea may be overly simple, but simple ideas are some of the most effective. Set an expectation around your routine for communicating with your families. Let them know exactly what type of communication to expect and when it will be communicated to them. For example, I send out a weekly newsletter to my families. In the newsletter, I always go over what the lesson content will be for the following week, reminders they need to know, and important links to information that needs to be communicated to them. I have also communicated that my newsletter will be emailed to them every Sunday afternoon. This helps me keep organized and parents always know when the newsletter is coming and what it will include.

For quick and easy-to-make newsletters, I use *Canva.com* and the editable templates they provide. Educators can access a premium account for free. They have pre-made newsletter templates that make it easy to format and plug in your information. I keep the formatting and template the same so families know how to navigate the newsletter. Also, by keeping the template and format the same, it makes it simple to update each week.

Offer Times to Connect - During the *Meet and Greet* one year, I had a parent approach me and say she was worried about the upcoming year because her daughter had a difficult time in third grade. She was distressed because her daughter thought she was the "bad" student teachers didn't like. First, there are no bad kids, just bad choices. Secondly, it sounded like this student was seeking connection and it was important that they feel connected. I let the parent know that I was invested in her child and that I would love the opportunity to sit down together the first week of school to discuss how we could work together to support her daughter. That meeting set myself, the student, and the family up for success because we started the year together knowing that we were all on the same page and on the same team.

During the *Meet and Greet* or *Back to School Night*, I am sure to let my families know that I would love the chance to sit down and talk about how, together, we can best help support their child. They can let me know in person, via e-mail, or write it down on the sheet they fill out to help me get to know their child a little better. I may only have a few families each year that take me up on scheduling such a meeting, but I am so grateful when they do because it always helps set a positive tone for the rest of the year.

This past year, because of COVID-19, I was unable to offer the same in-person meetings, so instead, I sent out a Google Form to families with the same questions, asking about their child and offering to set up a video call to touch base. This was a great way to connect with families that felt like they needed to connect or simply ask questions about what the year would look like. In the future, I plan to add a video conferencing option for families to allow for flexibility and access.

If a parent mentions that they're apprehensive about the upcoming year or communicate that they're worried about their child in one way or another, the best way to connect with families and partner with them for their child's success is to pick up the phone or schedule a meeting. These discussions may take a little bit of time, but they pay off in the long run because of the rapport you build, both with students and their families.

Student-Led Conferences - Conference time can bring about a lot of feelings among educators. It is exciting to have the opportunity to connect with families, but it can also be nerve-wracking not quite knowing what will be brought up or how to respond to questions from families. If you, as the educator, are feeling this way, you can bet that your students and their families may also have those feelings of uncertainty. When I first started teaching, I was told that our school did student-led conferences. I thought it was a wonderful idea, but I didn't quite know how to run them effectively, so I did what I thought was best at the time and wrote a sentence stem script for my students to fill in and read to their parents. It went something like this:

Hello _____, and welcome to my conference. My favorite thing about school is _____. I have enjoyed learning about _____. Something that is easy for me is _____. Something that is difficult for me is _____. My favorite book or story that we have read this year is _____. I would describe myself as _____. My goal for the year is _____.

The original script was longer and more detailed, but you get the picture. My thought was that students would fill in the missing information with their reflections about the year thus far and read the script to their families. Each conference season I would print off the sentence stem script and give it to my students before conferences so that they could fill it in and even practice reading it. The students complained about completing the script and practicing. Some didn't want to because they couldn't think of anything or didn't want to because they were bored.

Once conferences would happen, students would read their script to their families within five minutes and then I felt like I needed to fill the last fifteen minutes of the conferences with discussion about their reading and math scores and what all the numbers, letters, and scores meant. This was student-led, right? I guess it technically was, but neither the students nor their families were getting very much out of our time together. Everything changed one year when I read articles in one of my graduate programs about de-centering the school in what are supposed to be student- and family-centered events. This made me rethink everything I was doing with student-led conferences and how families experienced conferences. I needed to make them centered around what the students wanted to share and what the families wanted to hear about. I took the following steps to better meet the needs of my families during conferences and the feedback has been overwhelmingly positive:

School-Centered vs. Family-Centered

Many school events that we believe to be family-centered are actually school-centered events. In school-centered events, activities are determined by school staff or leaders: they decide what information to share, what activities will be done, and the format of the event. In school-centered events, the students and/or families have little-to-no say in the information, activities, and format. On the other hand, in a student and family-centered event, students and families have the opportunity to provide feedback about what information they are interested in hearing about, the activities that will be completed, and the format of the event. With this new lens, I started crafting student-led conferences that would truly be student-led and family centered.

Parent Feedback for Conferences

The first thing I did was reach out to families to learn more about their needs. I send out a very brief Google Form to families to find what they most want to hear about from their child. I try to keep these surveys short and to the point in order to make it easy on the families. These questions include:

1. Choose the top three things you are most interested in hearing about at conferences:

    a. Peer relationships

    b. Academic scores

    c. Academic extensions/supports

    d. Social emotional well-being

    e. Character traits shown during the school day

2. What is a question you would like me to answer?

    a. (Open-ended)

3. What is a question you would like your child to answer?

    a. (Open-ended)

4. Is there anything else you would like to tell me?

    a. (Open-ended)

In hindsight, it seems silly not to ask families what they are most interested in hearing about and it certainly changes at different times throughout the year. For example, during Fall conferences, the feedback from families I receive usually shows more interest in peer relationships and social emotional well-being after transitioning back to school. However, during winter conferences families usually show more interest in academic scores and supports/extensions. As educators, we want to make sure that we're reaching out and partnering with families to discover what information they are seeking.

Student-Generated Reflection Questions

Having students generate reflection questions might be my favorite part of student-led conferences. I take the data created from the Google Form sent out to parents (Google does a great job of putting the responses in graph form) and I share the responses with students. We look at which categories families wanted to hear most about, and which categories parents wanted to hear least about. Then, we focus on one category at a time and the students generate a list of reflection questions for each category.

First, I model what a reflection question from the category would sound like (examples of reflection questions below). Second, I have students discuss in a collaborative small group and come up with two to five questions that would help them reflect in each area. Once students create questions in their small collaborative groups, I have each group call out two or three of their favorite questions to share with the class. Then, I write all the questions on an anchor chart paper for that category. By the time we're done sharing, students will have created a list of 10 to 12 reflective questions for each category. Next, using the data, we decide how many questions from each category students should choose to reflect on. For example, if the feedback showed that more families were interested in hearing about the students' peer relationships, students would choose three to four questions from this category to reflect on and share with their families. However, for the categories that families were not as interested in, students may choose only one or two questions from these categories to reflect on.

Usually, if I send out five categories of interest to families, I'll have students choose three to four questions for the two categories parents are the most interested in, two to three questions for the next two categories, and finally one to two questions for the category families showed the least interest in hearing about. This is certainly flexible, and the number of questions can be changed based on what you and your students think.

This can also be differentiated for students who may need modified work. To do this, I would sit down individually with students who needed to scaffold or modify the number of questions and go through each category with them and choose the number of questions they feel comfortable reflecting on. Sometimes, we just choose the questions together then and there to help them get started. Again, because they get to choose which questions, they reflect on, there is instant engagement to complete the task. However, chunking it into manageable portions for students can help make this experience even more positive for them.

What I love most about this practice is that you are looking at the feedback data with your students, discussing what categories families were most interested in versus which categories families were not as interested in, and taking that information to help students make decisions around what their families want to hear from them at conferences. I also love that the students are the ones generating their own reflection questions and they have the agency to choose which questions they want to reflect on. This agency immediately increases engagement because they are the ones choosing what they want to share and reflect on with family members.

Examples to consider when generating questions:

Peer Relationships: Do my friendships have a positive impact on me? Are my friends kind to me?

Academic Scores: What skills/subjects do I feel confident about? What skills/subjects do I want to improve on?

Academic Extensions/Supports: What tools do I use to help me succeed in the classroom? What do I need to challenge myself academically?

Social Emotional Well-Being: What is something that brings me joy throughout the day? Is there anything that makes me feel anxious or nervous during the day?

Character Traits: What character traits do I think I exhibit each day? What is one character trait I want to focus on?

Front Loading Data

Before changing my conferences into authentically family-centered and student-led events, I would spend at least ten minutes of precious conference time explaining to families what all the data and numbers meant academically for their child. Not only was this wasting time that could be used for them to ask questions, but it also didn't give the families time to process the meaning of it all to be able to ask informed questions or voice concerns they may have.

So, I decided to frontload families with their child's data by sending home a data sheet with all their scores and annual growth goals on it (iReady reading and math, DIBELS, and DRA2) before conferences. Then, I would send out a video explaining what all the numbers meant, what the benchmark was for this time in the year and how their annual growth goal was determined. No longer was I wasting time during conferences doing the explaining, but instead having important conversations with families about their children's academic success or my plans to continue to support and grow their abilities. By sending out this information early, I was giving families the tools they needed to understand where their children were performing academically and have the time to process and come prepared with any questions they had.

Conference Creation

To continue supporting student agency, I allowed students to choose the medium in which they would like to present for their families. They could choose to use technology and create a presentation on an online platform/app or choose an in-person medium.

Here are some of the choices they have:

Technology Mediums:
+ Keynote
+ Google Slides
+ Prezi

- Powtoon
- Book Creator
- Canva
- Video Blog
- Green Screen Video
- Pixton

In-Person Mediums:
- Picture book
- Poster
- Script to read (created completely by the student)
- Collage
- Comic strip

Once they choose a medium, they focus on selecting the reflection questions from the list brainstormed by the class. This is also the time I give individual students the specific questions their families posed to them via their survey if they had any. They can present their reflections to these questions in any way they want using their chosen medium as long as they are explanatory. We discuss the difference between giving a one-word answer and explaining the answer—mainly they need to tell their parents the *why* behind their answer.

Some students will need this modeled for them. For example, if a student were answering the question, "Do my friendships have a positive impact on me?" and they just answer "Yes," encourage them to offer an example showing how they have a good impact on them to explain the "why" behind their answer. I model changing that "Yes." to "Yes, because when I fell down during recess, they came to help me up and made sure that I was all right." This not only answers the question, but it explains *why* as well. Check-in with students about their conference creations by asking them what they are most excited about sharing or what was the most difficult question to reflect on. This will help you understand how your students are doing with the presentation and if they may need more support in completing it.

Practice Makes Perfect

If you're a teacher and have sat through conferences, then you've experienced that some of your most outspoken students in the classroom become timid and quiet when their family is in the same room with you! It's amazing how their demeanor changes and they suddenly become nervous because their two worlds are suddenly colliding. To prepare your students for their conference, give them time to practice presenting or leading their conference. This can be done with you (the teacher) or a partner. Giving your students the opportunity to practice will help them feel more comfortable when they get in front of both you and their family to lead their conference.

Conference Time

Finally, on conference day, make sure your students have what they need to lead and feel successful. Encourage them to take charge because they're running the show. By this point, they are usually very excited to share their work with their families. Unless they need me, I simply welcome their family into our classroom and give the student the floor. Once their presentation is over, I compliment them on their hard work and then turn my attention to their family and ask if they have any questions for the student or me. This gives the family time to have their questions answered, centering them in the conferences.

This process allows everyone to come to conferences and know exactly what to expect. You, as the teacher, will likely know what questions your families are coming in with from the survey, your students will be the ones presenting the information being discussed, and your families are the ones who have voiced what they wanted to hear about and know what to expect to hear at the conference.

Student-Led Conference Odds and Ends

First, conferences should be about celebrating student work. This means that families should not be hearing concerns you have about their child for the first time at conferences. Rather, any concerns you have about the student should be voiced to families prior to conferences and either discussed at a different time or discussed prior to the student-led conference. Remember, this should be a positive experience for both your student and their family because it is an important part of building trust and rapport. You do not want to tarnish the trust built with a student by bringing up new concerns about them without having front-loaded the family of your concerns first.

Second, the prep work for this process *seems* daunting, but once you have the bones of what to send out, each conference season becomes easier because you can use the same templates and videos to send out to families. I've even got a Google Form template for the family interest form made up for you to use. Head to https://bit.ly/3ff1AKH to make a forced copy for your Google Drive.

Third, the thing I hear most about from teachers is not having time to do this in class. I understand that time in the classroom is incredibly precious. However, I implore you to think about the power of student reflection on their work and how impactful it is for them to honestly assess how they are doing in your classroom. Reflection is an important tool for students to be able to utilize in order to improve their learning and have ownership over that improvement. To make the most of our time, I usually take about fifteen minutes as a whole group to introduce student-led conferences and the process we will embark on together. Then, once parent feedback is in, I take about thirty minutes as a whole group to look at the feedback and generate questions together. At the end of that thirty minutes, I have students decide which medium they would like to use in order to create their student-led presentation. From there, the rest of the work is independent. This is work that students do while they are not in a small group with me during our intervention time over the course of two weeks. I suggest outlining a timeline of what needs to be completed by when over the course of those two weeks so that students have an idea of how to manage their time. I also find time throughout those two weeks to check-in with students to see where they are at and if they need any support.

By shifting our conference structure to become more family-centered, we are showing our students' families that we want to partner with them, we value their opinions, and we want to ensure they are getting the information they are looking for. Even if student-led conferences are not the norm in your building, reach out to your administration and explain the power of this structure. Ask if you can try it out in your room and see how it goes. A small pilot can be a powerful tool to show the rest of the school how great an idea can be.

Contacting Home for Good News - This next section is one, admittedly, I am always working on. I think most teachers and families subscribe to the idea that no news is good news and although that may be true at times, letting families know that their child is doing well is just as important as contacting home to ask for support. Taking the time to contact home to express a celebration or simply letting their family know that their child is doing a great job in class can go a long way in establishing a mutual culture of trust and respect between teachers and families.

As educators, we have so much on our plate that adding one more thing feels like it could be too much. However, what if we broke it up? What if we decided to send 3-5 emails each week (maybe even just one a day) telling a family things you notice their child doing well, something amazing they did for a friend, or something they have significantly improved on? Now we've taken the daunting task of sending 30+ emails in one sitting to sending just one a day. Families will hear from their teacher every few weeks with an update on something positive about their child. How great is that? If you can find the time to call—that is even better. Those calls are usually short, but so sweet. This build up in rapport shows families that you are looking at their whole child and finding the things that they do well or are working hard on. You are seeing the good in each one of them, which is an important lens for every educator to use. This relationship is so important for when hard calls must be made to ask for help in supporting their child. Families will know when you're on their team in supporting their child because they know you see the good in them and want them to thrive and be successful.

Flames in the Classroom #4

Krystal Smith

Krystal is a fourth and fifth grade math and social studies teacher in Pittsburgh, Pennsylvania. Here, Krystal explains ways that she connects and builds relationships with her students' families:

The families of our students are our biggest allies. I don't just tell families I believe we are on the same team, I *show* them. I recruit them. I thank them. I support them. I invite them to my room at any given time. Even this year, teaching remotely, I have called families to the computer to discuss the progress of their children or even just to sit in on a lesson. I value them. I let them know, upfront, that I cannot help their child be successful without their support and input. Teamwork makes the dreamwork.

There are many things I do to build community and rapport with the families of my students. The three I will share all occur before your students even enter your classroom. About a week before school starts, I mail letters home to families. Yes, that's a lot of paper, ink, stamps, envelopes, and time (Hopefully, your school can help with the financial part). The letter introduces me, my experience, and my expectations. I also include the grade level, homeroom, the date for Back-to-School Night, and the first day of school date in the letter. I have even mailed letters to my new students, too. Kids love receiving mail with their names on it!

In addition to the letter, the second thing I do is include an opportunity for families to respond. They can respond by writing me a letter and bringing it to the school on Back-to-School Night, or by having their child bring it to school on the first day of school. In more recent years, I have also sent links to a Google Form to record responses. Here is the catch: When they respond, I am very clear on what I want them to write about. I only want families to share positive thoughts. I want them to tell me everything good about their child. I want to see the joy they see. I want to see the love they have for their child. This is my favorite part because I immediately have families thinking positively, which influences how I perceive their child before they even enter my room. If they had a bad reputation last year, I am offered a new perspective, and an opportunity to see a child in a different light. This is important. Many teachers often wonder how a student they taught the previous year is now a completely different child when they enter my class the following year. I try to get a bigger picture of who they are and work it to my advantage. There is at least one child every year about whom a teacher can't believe, "That is the same child!?"

Of course, I get information from former teachers, and usually it includes the good, the bad, and the ugly. However, I use the positive information, again, to my advantage. On the first day of school, I have something authentic to talk to them about. Later in the year, when or if a student is beginning to show behaviors that bother me and their classmates, disrupting the classroom culture, community building, and learning that happens, I re-read these letters to help me see this child as their family sees them. Typically, my initial response towards the child changes, and "just like magic," their behavior is better. Let's be clear. It's not magic. It's all about rapport and respect.

The last thing I do is call families to follow up with the letters. Most times I don't speak to every family, but I do leave voice messages and/or send text messages. This last step is important because the first phone call home was a "good news" phone call home. One of the best tips I can share with any teacher is to always make sure the first phone call to families is a positive phone call. It allows the families to trust you and be more receptive when you do have to make a phone call bearing not-so-good news. Don't be afraid to connect with families because families are our biggest allies. Reach out early to build community and rapport. This is laying the foundation for success.

Connect with Krystal:
Instagram: @the_renewed_teacher
Twitter: @RenewEDTeacher
Facebook: The Renewed Teacher
Blog: www.renewedteacher.com
Teachers Pay Teachers: The RenewED Teacher

Bringing Families In to Share Their Expertise

As a teacher, I'm always looking for ways to bring content to life in the classroom. One of the best ways I've found to bring content to life is by inviting family members to come in and lead a lesson or share with the class about their area of work or expertise. I've always put this out to families during back-to-school night, during the meet and greet, and in newsletters. I want families to know that they are valued and can bring valuable life and real-world experience into our classroom.

One year, I had a parent who was passionate about space. He visited our classroom to teach a lesson about the size of our solar system. He took the class outside and created a life-size scale model of the solar system with the students so they could see first-hand how large our solar system is and the varying space between all the planets. It was an experience they all remembered for the remainder of the year. He also had a large telescope and worked with my grade-level team to put on star-gazing nights over the years, during which students and their families could come out to the school on a clear night and see the different constellations and any celestial objects that were in view. We were able to use this parent's expertise to build a strong relationship with that family for years to come, but also have other students benefit from his knowledge.

Another year, I had a mom who was an astronomy professor contact me and ask if she could come in and do a lesson for our sun, moon, and stars unit, to which I gleefully agreed. She led multiple hands-on activities with students to show the distance between Earth and the moon, the moon phases, and she even taught students how to make sundials. I was incredibly grateful that this amazing mom was able to offer my students this memorable experience.

I've also had parents who are real estate agents or financial advisors come in during our personal financial literacy unit to discuss the importance of financial literacy in the real world. One year, a mom who was a financial advisor taught a lesson on the stock market and showed how it worked. She tied it to the concepts of opportunity cost and scarcity which were terms we learned about in our curriculum. She provided real-world examples of scarcity and cost in action. She also explained the role stocks can play in helping people save for the future—I learned a few things myself that day!

Another year a mother who was also a real estate agent came in and taught a lesson on budgeting and it was a hit. She put the students into groups and gave each group a profession with an average annual income (without tax). Then, the students had to solve to find how much money each profession would make each month and create a budget for rent/mortgage payments, car payments, gas, groceries, etc. I will never forget the group assigned to be teachers because as soon as they started budgeting, they said, "Oh my gosh, there is hardly anything left over to do fun things like go to the movies! Ms. Saeed, is this true?" All I could do was laugh because it was the truth! Again, I was so thankful that this mom had asked to come in and did this lesson because budgeting is an important real-life skill.

Bringing families in and sharing their wealth of knowledge and passions with the students has been an incredibly positive experience. As a teacher, I am constantly reminding my students that I do not know everything—it may seem that way sometimes to them, but there is so much out there that I don't know. I cannot be a master at everything, but I can reach out and find people who are masters of their content and are willing to share with the class. If you haven't tried to reach out to families to come into the classroom, I highly suggest putting it out there. Some years, no one comes in and other years I have multiple people volunteer. Regardless of who can come in, by extending the invitation you are showing that families are welcome in your classroom. Experiences like these are possible because of the relationships that have been forged over the course of the year. Without this relationship, families might feel like you're checking a box rather than truly being invested in what they can bring to the table. These relationships help portray your authenticity in partnering with them as valued experts.

Relationships Built for a Lifetime

When teachers and schools build relationships with families, they can last a lifetime. There is a special bond that occurs between families and teachers when they truly see how much you care for their children. That care doesn't stop when that student leaves your classroom to move onto the next grade; it continues forever. There are times when I stop and think, "I wonder how that student is doing," and that's because we are never done caring for our students. We carry each student in our hearts for a lifetime and it's a bonus when a strong enough relationship is built with families that they become friends for years to come.

I have been fortunate enough to build these bonds with a few families over the years and it truly fills me with joy when I am able to catch up and connect with them. Some students who are voracious readers still reach out, even years later, and ask for recommendations for book series to read. These students, in turn, have given me recommendations as well—I even had one go as far as to bring me a stack of her own books to borrow because she knew I would take good care of them and wanted me to read the series (In case you're wondering, it was the *Lunar Chronicles* by Marissa Meyer and it was, indeed, fantastic).

I've also had the pleasure of hosting past students as volunteers in my classroom during the year and over the summer. I've also been lucky enough to still be able to meet up with parents of former students to discuss the books we've read, swap must-read titles, and talk about how amazing their kids are and the incredible people they are growing up to become. These connections and relationships I absolutely cherish because it lasts longer than the single short school year that we have together.

Putting the time and energy into developing rapport with families is critical to the success of our students. I think of the teacher-family relationship as a partnership or team: We are working together to support students to feel and be successful in the classroom. Sometimes, this can't be done alone on our end at school—sometimes we need the support of families to give a student what they need to be successful. As educators, we can cultivate these important relationships through consistent communication and positive interactions with families. Remember to let them know how much you care, remember to let them know that you see the good in their child, and remember to let them know that you are on the same team.

> Putting the time and energy into developing rapport with families is critical to the success of our students.

Be the Flame Actions

Reflect on how you have built rapport with families from past years, asking yourself these questions:

- What have I done in the past that has successfully built rapport with families?
- What could I add in to bolster these relationships?
- How can I keep my family communication consistent and inclusive?

- Are my conferences family-centered? If not, what changes could I adopt to make them more family-centered?
- What steps can I take to ensure I am sending home positive individual communication on a consistent basis?

CHAPTER 6

Fuel

A teacher's support system is the *Fuel* that powers their flame. Building positive rapport and connections with other educators in the school is essential to receiving ongoing support throughout each day.

"Unity is strength. When there is teamwork and collaboration, wonderful things can be achieved."

– Mattie Stepanek

Building Community with Teammates

Teaching is a fulfilling and rewarding profession; we are able to work with students and help shape the amazing people they become. It is also a profession that is exhausting and isolating at times. The support of a grade level or school team is critical to the success and belonging of teachers. Teacher contracts outline a six- to seven-hour workday, but in reality, teachers are working for hours before and after school and on their weekends and holidays. In some schools, this work is done in isolation, leaving the teacher feeling alone and as if they are battling to swim upstream with no help. As educators, it is imperative that we are creating relationships with our teammates that fuel us and build a system of support to avoid burnout. Creating a culture of trust and collaboration among a team is paramount to the success of a school. School teams should be a built-in support system for all teachers. It takes time and care to cultivate and maintain these relationships, but the results are well worth the time and investment.

I have been fortunate to be part of some amazing and supportive teams over my teaching career. Without their support and guidance, I have to wonder where I would be in my professional career. Although my team has changed incrementally each and every year I've taught, we have always found ways to connect and bond in order to create a support system among ourselves. I have been on teams with five grade level teachers and teams with three (including myself), and the common denominator is that we trust and support each other unconditionally. We always assume positive intent in one another which helps us navigate conversations about values, data, and teaching strategies.

This trust isn't built overnight, and it takes work to maintain, but we put that work in together so that when we need each other most, we are there. In time, we have become more than a team, we have become a family.

This system of support is always important, especially when the unimaginable happens. We have supported each other through the passing of loved ones, sickness, hospitalization, and the illness of family members. I know, from experience, that if something happened tomorrow and I was unable to make it to school that my team would take over no questions asked, because that's what families do.

We are a support system for one another, but we are cheerleaders as well. Together, we celebrate accomplishments and successes. We laugh and joke *a lot* which is an important part of our bond. Some days we vent, but mainly we remind each other of the joy that happens each day. Best of all, we are all very different people, experiencing life in different capacities and bringing our individual lenses to the team.

During the first couple weeks of my first-year teaching, we had moved past team- and community-building lessons and were ready to jump into teaching content. The first couple years I was at my school, there was not a scripted literacy curriculum. Rather, it was open-ended for teachers to use any resources they wanted, and we built units ourselves as long as the lessons were connected directly to the standards. As a veteran teacher, the flexibility and space for creativity sounds amazing. However, as a first-year teacher fresh out of student teaching, I was terrified. I felt as if I had forgotten everything I had learned in my education classes and student teaching. I forgot how to plan a lesson by looking at the standards and working backwards from an assessment. I forgot how to find appropriate grade level texts. I was a deer in headlights when it came to planning a reading lesson.

Fortunately, I was paired with a mentor who I confided in, and she suggested observing one of my teammates. She offered to step in and teach a lesson in my classroom while I went to do an observation. We had only known each other for about a month at this point, but I approached one of my teammates and asked if she would feel comfortable with me observing her reading lesson. I explained that I was struggling to structure my reading block and would love the opportunity to see what she is doing in her room. Without hesitation, my teammate invited me into her classroom and offered to meet with me before or after school to go over what her entire reading block looked like and how she planned her lessons. I am so thankful she welcomed me into her classroom, and I will never forget that observation because I learned so much that day.

From then on, I knew that I did not have to struggle in silence or isolation; all I needed to do was reach out and ask for help. When I asked, it was always there. Often, we fear that we may be burdening or bothering our teammates; however, if we take the time to build a community among our teammates, we know that we will never have to struggle alone.

Quality Time

Finding time to slow down and spend time together is important for building relationships with your teammates. Getting to know each other as people and the lives we all have outside of school helps you understand who your teammates are and the wealth of knowledge outside of education that they bring to the team.

Team Breakfasts

During my first year, we formed a brand-new team in the fourth grade. Two of my teammates had worked together the year before, but two of us were new hires. There was an administrative policy in place at the time, requiring us to meet as a grade level team once a month to discuss pacing and content (which seems crazy now because we meet at least once a week to plan and pace together). My team didn't think it was enough time to get to know each other, especially since two of us were located in the building and the other two were located outside in portable classrooms. One of my teammates suggested we meet weekly to touch base and connect. Thus, the weekly "Friday Breakfast" was born!

Each week, we would rotate bringing breakfast in for the whole team. Whoever was bringing breakfast that morning would host the breakfast in their room. We met an hour before school started to eat and chat. We used this time on Friday mornings to talk about the week and laugh about the ups and downs. These breakfasts created a fast track for us to get to know each other as individuals and truly bond as a team.

Lunch

Over the years, lunch together has been an on again, off again event. Sometimes things come up throughout the day and lunch time is the only time to take care of them—personal or professional. Over the years, I have eaten my lunch in my classroom where I listen to music or a podcast and unwind and rejuvenate for the rest of the day. However, this year has changed that routine and we cannot be in our classrooms during lunch time because they are being cleaned (remember, I'm writing this while teaching through the COVID-19 pandemic). Luckily, living in Colorado, if it's not snowing, it's usually sunny. Therefore, my team and I have been enjoying lunch outside together this year. We even invested in our own camping chairs and bring them outside to the front of the school and space ourselves ten feet apart to enjoy our lunch while talking about our day. I thought that I would miss my podcasts and catching up on work during my lunch time, but it turns out connecting with my team during lunch has brought me so much more joy. We are able to discuss how lessons played out in our different classrooms, we troubleshoot engagement issues we're seeing with students, and—best of all—share the funny stories that come from working with kids.

Make Time to Have Fun Together

A few years ago, our school created "Pride Awards." If a student was going above and beyond school expectations, you could write them a pride award for their awesome behavior. Once you wrote a pride award, you would turn a copy of it into the front office so that they could be read out loud by our principal on the morning announcements.

Our team thought it would be funny to sneak a pride award in each week that recognized a famous musician, athlete, or artist and then say that they did a great job in music, PE, or art. One Pride Award read: Harry Styles was recognized for "Doing a great job in music!"

Our school is a movement school and on Friday mornings the entire school gets together for the first twenty minutes of the day and participates in what is called *All School Movement*. This is where all the kids participate in guided dance or Tabata exercises to get them moving and ready to take on the last day of the week. If you are a regular consumer of *GoNoodle* (a brain break website) you probably know the famous duo Koo Koo Kangaroo. The previous year our team had dressed up as Koo Koo Kangaroo for Halloween and when we heard that the All School Movement theme one Friday was going to be Koo Koo Kangaroo songs, we jumped at the opportunity to bring Koo Koo Kangaroo to life. That morning, we came dressed as Koo Koo Kangaroo and danced as backup dancers to the teachers who were guiding the entire school in the dance. The best part was that some of the students really thought Koo Koo Kangaroo had come to our school for All School Movement. It's the little things that bond teams together. We must find the small joys and simple ways to bring fun and happiness into what we do.

Flames in the Classroom #5

Juan E. Gonzalez

Juan is a third-grade teacher in League City, Texas. Here, Juan explains one way he and his team stay connected and find time to spend together:

Behind the veil of a classroom, there are humans working together to achieve success in strengthening growing learners. I learned early in my career that the work of education cannot be experienced alone. Having strong relationships with co-workers inside a school building can create the magic that brings us all to this profession. The magic looks different for everyone, but I believe it all sits on a foundation of hope. Working together happens best when you let people show up as themselves.

When building relationships with my co-workers, I always speak, support, and listen with respect. Everyone in our school buildings comes from different backgrounds. We're also working with various challenges in the classroom. We must see and hear each other completely. When we're continuously problem solving our personal classroom challenges, it's easy to develop tunnel vision of our own journey. During staff meetings, team meetings, and passing conversations, remind yourself that your work is a piece to the big puzzle and that we need each other.

The work we do is serious, but finding moments of fun can bring you closer to your team. At the beginning of each school year, our grade level team comes together to create team norms for holidays and birthdays. This allows everyone to share a piece of themselves and establish some traditions that feel fresh each school year. One of the best team celebrations I experienced was when we decided that once a month, we would order out for lunch, and have it delivered to the school. Regardless of the status of our school day or the amount of time we had to eat, we promised to always enjoy this meal together. After a failed lesson, a bad day, or just the simple desire to disconnect from the teaching world for a moment, having a special lunch together established a bond that only food can create.

Remember to assume the best about everyone in your school building. The decision to work in education is rarely a career that someone stumbles upon. We choose education for various reasons, with the common thread being to serve our community. This small connection between all of us in education is something that always warms my heart. Humanizing my colleagues and believing the best in their intentions allows for communication and respect to blossom. When I make the conscious effort to adopt this positive mindset, I am more likely to give words of encouragement and supportive feedback. We can't expect everyone to be their best if we don't believe them.

This profession is hard work and cannot be done alone. Listen, respect, and support—with all your heart.

Connect with Juan:
Instagram: @teaching3rdwithmrg
Facebook: Teaching 3rd with Mr G
Teachers Pay Teachers: Teaching 3rd with Mr. G

Our Students

My school has worked really hard on shifting the idea from we should only be worrying about the students within our classrooms or on our roster to all students within the school are *our* students. This paradigm shift has allowed our teams to open up and discuss the needs of all students to better meet the needs of students within all classrooms. It can feel frustrating when we have exhausted all the strategies in our teacher toolbox with one student and nothing seems to be helping that student succeed. As teachers, we tend to take these moments very personally because we feel we have not been able to provide the support that a student needs. Reaching out to your team during these moments is crucial and necessary to (hopefully) be provided ideas and a perspective that you may have been unable to see on your own. By seeking the support and know-how of our teammates, we may just discover an idea we have yet to try that could make all the difference.

I really pride myself on being able to connect with almost any student who has entered my classroom. That includes meeting the individual academic and social emotional needs of all students. One year, I had a student who needed extra support learning how to collaborate in a group setting. I felt that I had tried everything in my teacher toolbox with this student to help them positively collaborate with their group, but nothing seemed to work. Rather than continue to try strategies that were not helping the student succeed, I decided to reach out to her teacher from the previous year as well as a teacher this student worked with one-on-one to pick their brains for ideas to help the student be successful.

The teacher who had this student the previous year suggested creating a job or role for her to focus on and use while collaborating when in a group. The teacher that worked one-on-one with the student suggested creating a positive incentive system where this student could work towards rewards that they chose. Those were two ideas I had not yet implemented, and I was extremely grateful that they were able to give me some new ideas to use with this student.

I ended up implementing both ideas by creating a role for the student when she worked in a group setting and, together, the student and I discussed what it would look like if she were being successful in her group fulfilling her role responsibilities. Each time she was able to show the collaborative behaviors we outlined in her group, she was positively incentivized with cooperation cash which she could trade in for school-based rewards (having a lunch bunch with three friends, ten minutes of free draw time, ten minutes of iPad time, etc.) that she chose. Within a couple of weeks this student was able to positively interact with her group and after a month, the student no longer needed the positive incentive system because she was intrinsically motivated to be a part of and work with her group.

Had I not reached out to these teachers to gain their perspective and ideas in supporting this student, I wonder what would have become of that year. Would both the student and I have been incredibly frustrated the entire year? Would the student have been able to gain the collaborative skills that she needed? The great thing is, I never had to find out because I sought out the expertise of professionals within my building. When we see the students in our school as *our* kids rather than mine and yours, we create a culture in which *all* teachers can be involved in the success of *all* students.

Direct Conversations

Again, this may be an overly simple idea, but make sure you're having direct conversations with teammates or co-workers when needed. No one enjoys conflict, but sometimes having an uncomfortable and direct conversation with a co-worker can help avoid further controversy and hurt. If there is something that occurs between you and a co-worker or teammate that calls for the air to be cleared, then having a conversation can help rebuild a relationship that may have been damaged. I've said it once and I'll say it again: I am not an expert. Direct conversations are not my forte, but I do know from experience that having a direct conversation with someone with whom you have a conflict will help move both of you forward in mending your relationship.

> No one enjoys conflict, but sometimes having an uncomfortable and direct conversation with a co-worker can help avoid further controversy and hurt.

Find Your People

Finding your people refers to finding other people in your system that you get along with and who share your personal and/or professional values. They are the people you turn to when you need to be reenergized, get a different perspective on an issue, or talk out a problem you may be facing. These people may be outside of your immediate team, which is why it's important to get to know the other staff members in your building.

Getting to know other staff members can be difficult with all the differing grade level schedules, but there are a few things you can do to branch out and get to know more people. Try joining a committee or leadership team of interest to you. This gives you the ability to meet a variety of staff members who are all interested in supporting the school in the same way as you. You can also encourage your administrators to do quick team building activities during staff meetings in vertical teams so that you have the opportunity to work with teachers from different grade levels. Finally, consider eating in the teachers' lounge with colleagues you normally do not interact with. If there are overlapping lunch schedules, you may be able to cross paths with a staff member that you don't normally run into. If you're a veteran teacher in your building, consider reaching out to the first-year teachers and new hires as much as possible. They may be looking for their people and you may find a friend in them as well.

There are many different metaphors for finding people within your organization or school that help you grow and flourish as a person and professional. One of those metaphors is the marigold. Marigolds, when planted next to other plants, help them to grow strong and healthy. Jennifer Gonzalez from *The Cult of Pedagogy* podcast (2013) encourages teachers to find their "marigolds" in the workplace, meaning, finding co-workers who share your vision and passion and who help you thrive in the school setting. Finding your people is a vital component of building a support system and community to help you flourish as a teacher.

Another metaphor I have heard used is from *Powerful Teaching* (2019) author Patrice Bain. She uses poppies to explain how to connect with others who share your educational vision. Poppies in a garden that are all the same size don't see very many differences among one another. However, some poppies that go above and beyond might become taller than the others. Tall poppies have a more difficult time finding a support system because they are seemingly different from the others. It's important that tall poppies seek to find other tall poppies because they share the same values and vision. Find other tall poppies who are supporting one another and encourage each other to stand tall.

I have found both of these metaphors to be extremely relevant, especially in education. It is life changing to find people who support your success unconditionally because they know that your success does not hinder their ability to be successful as well. The love and support that I have found with "my people" in my system will last a lifetime because that support moves from your professional life and seeps into your personal life. They celebrate your successes and prop you up when you are in danger of wilting. In turn, you champion them as they have championed you, because that is what support systems do.

Having a partner and/or family that is supportive of the teaching profession is important, but finding a support system of people who are in the trenches with you and understand the ins-and-outs and ups and downs of our reality can be exponentially helpful.

Be the Flame Actions

Reflect on how you have built community with your team and/or co-workers from past years, and consider the following:

- What is my current relationship with my teammates? Is there anything that we can implement that would help us grow our rapport?
- Plan a team meal where you eat together and spend time checking in with one another.
- If you're feeling tension with a teammate, plan a time to have a direct conversation with them to work towards a solution.

CHAPTER 7

Spread

Sharing and learning with others is essential to our continued growth as educators. We must *Spread* our flames.

"In a world of algorithms, hashtags, and followers, know the true importance of human connection."

– Simi Fromen

Finding an Online Community

If someone told me ten years ago that I would have established strong friendships with people across the world on a social media platform, I would have thought they were crazy. In fact, I didn't even have an Instagram account ten years ago. Fast forward to today and I have been able to see what a dynamic tool social media can be.

I first started my teaching Instagram account in 2016 as a way to record my journey of moving out of the building into a portable classroom and starting flexible seating. I had also decided to start a Teachers Pay Teachers account and thought that Instagram would be a great place to show other educators the resources I had created. At that time, I was ecstatic that anywhere from six to ten people I did not know were looking at my classroom pictures and liking my photos.

The following year I made the effort to post regularly throughout the school year and through those posts I was able to engage with more teachers via comments and direct messages. Since then, my teacher account has grown in size, and I have had the opportunity to connect with many fantastic educators (like the *Flames in the Classroom* who shared their voices throughout this book). I was amazed that the online teaching community is truly worldwide. Educators from around the globe use Instagram and Twitter to share their knowledge, classroom ideas, organizational tips, and so much more. Finding an online teaching community can be a powerful tool for belonging, connection, and miniature professional development.

In the early 2000's AIM was big and platforms like Xenga and MySpace attracted people of all kinds. I remember my parents warning me about chat rooms and adding friends on MySpace that I didn't know. Then, a couple years ago I did the one thing that my parents told me never to do: meeting up with people that I met on the internet!

I had cultivated a friendship with a couple of teachers on Instagram. We shared a lot of the same content and used each other's ideas in the classroom. They were like teammates who I had never met in-person. Each of us lived in a different state and it didn't seem likely that we would ever meet. There was a teaching conference all three of us were interested in going to and we decided that it would be a great place for us to meet up. One of the teachers had family in the area who were willing to host us while we were in town, so we booked flights, made sub plans, and traveled across the country to attend the conference together. I felt like I took a leap of faith by flying out to Charlotte, North Carolina, to meet these teachers who I didn't know personally. They shared my same educational vision and passion for education and when we finally met face-to-face, the chemistry between the three of us was instant. It was as if we had known each other our entire lives. The conference was rejuvenating and I'm so glad that I was able to experience it with these two teachers who shared the same drive and passion for our profession.

Other connections I've made on Instagram have resulted in friendships that span over years. There are people who I text and talk with regularly who I have never met before but are an amazing support system for me. There are people I connect with regularly on Instagram who reach out during difficult times to see how I am holding up or send encouraging messages to celebrate good news. There are amazing people I have "met" through social media who I consider friends. Instagram friends can definitely be real world friends, even if thousands of miles separate us. It's incredible the connections and community that can be created through an online platform.

Flames in the Classroom #6

Kaitlin Johnstone

Kaitlin is a kindergarten teacher and founder of "Kind Cotton" in Bradenton, Florida. Here, Kaitlin shares how she has used social media to connect with educators across the globe to spread her mission of putting books in the hands of children:

Every great educator shares a common characteristic: Creating a community of learning in which children feel loved, valued, and seen. I have spent seven years in the classroom; 6 of those 7 were in Kindergarten and I loved every moment because I had the opportunity to make or break a child's relationship with school. Teachers are given this extraordinary chance of establishing an environment based upon strong relationships to help their students thrive emotionally as well as academically. Seeing the growth and developing those connections are at the core of education, but so often teachers are spending the bulk of their day with only children. They aren't necessarily able to create a community among one another due to lack of time.

It was not until four years ago when we started our business, *Kind Cotton*, a clothing company focused on redefining kindness and putting books in the hands of children nationwide, that I truly understood the need to create a safe space for educators to connect. Along came Instagram, and the rest is history. At the core of our company is a love of reading, a natural fit for most educators. As we started sharing stories about the books we were donating, more and more teachers began following our page. Never did I imagine that our company that tangibly gives back to children would also emotionally give back to adults. Social media can absolutely be dangerous, a space in which one compares themselves to a perfectly crafted reel of flawlessness without seeing the struggles that take place when the phones are turned off. However, if approached authentically, social media can also be inspiring.

We have connected with thousands of educators across the globe and discussed things as simple as our favorite Starbucks order all the way to the depths of redefining kindness in such a way that it must involve justice and inclusion. We have realized through our work that human connection is the key to everything. When I sit down each day to look at my phone and post our next story or product, I am not just selling to our followers; I am engaging in dialogue. I am painting a picture. I am connecting with their very real emotions whether they be joy, hope, or sadness. Human beings crave connection, and they crave connection that is rooted in trust. I truly feel that being a Kindergarten teacher, who knew exactly how to help my children feel welcomed and loved, has helped me build an online community in which adults feel safe, appreciated, and bonded to one another. It's about being there, being real, and being open. It's about finding ways to become change makers with like-minded people. As with anything in life, if you want to make an impact, you must give it your undivided attention. Attention equals love and when someone feels that, they buy in.

Connect with Kaitlin:
Instagram: @kindcotton
Facebook: Kind Cotton
Website: www.kindcotton.com

Professional Learning Networks

A professional learning network (PLN) allows you to invest and engage with an online community in your professional realm. You can use social media platforms such as Twitter, Instagram, Facebook, and even TikTok to connect with educators who are sharing what they are doing in the classroom, learning in professional development, or having open dialogue about best practices. Better yet, you can use it to share what *you're* doing in the classroom. My professional learning network is a staple in my practice and the content that I engage in has taught me a variety of things that I use in my classroom daily. From engagement strategies to conceptual math practices to the science of reading, I am constantly learning and taking in new information that is making me a better educator.

Scrolling your professional learning network is like a miniature professional development. I know most people think of platforms like Instagram as places where teachers only take pictures of their daily outfits and classroom decor. However, I would push back on that notion and say it depends on who you follow. I can scroll through my Instagram feed, which I have carefully curated over the years and instantly pick up a few ideas for my classroom. In my most recent "saved" posts, I can find information on picture books about fossils I would like to add to my classroom library, a professional development book I want to order on the science of reading, a video on how to encourage problem solving through drawing in math, and a tech tool that I plan to investigate using with my students. I work to fill my feed with educators who are sharing information that helps me grow and is not just aesthetically pleasing.

If you're interested in building your professional learning network, I highly suggest searching hashtags on each platform to find educational creators with content that resonates with you. Hashtags are similar to keywords which help you find content and creators in the professional realm of your choice. Here are some examples:

Educational Instagram hashtags: #Teaching #Education #TeacherLife #ITeachToo #TeachersOfInstagram

Educational Twitter hashtags: #EdChat #Edu #Education #EduChat #Teachers

Educational TikTok hashtags: #Teacher #TeacherTok #TeachersOfTikTok #TikTokTeacher

Starting a professional learning network doesn't mean you have to become a social media master overnight. I suggest starting small and finding educational creators who encourage you to grow. Find other accounts that have content that spark your thinking and possibly provide resources for your classroom. It can feel daunting to comment or message someone, but don't be afraid to connect because that is how rapport is built. Building relationships online takes time, but if you put the effort in (just like in-person relationships) they start to flourish.

Finally, it's not about the number of followers someone has or the number of followers you have. It's about finding other individuals who share the same love for education as you. To start curating your feed, use hashtags to find more accounts, look at who is liking and commenting on posts you liked or found helpful, and look at accounts that you like and see who they are following. It starts small, but you will find that there are so many wonderful educators out there who are excited to connect and grow together.

Find People Who Challenge Your Thinking

I mention that it's important to find and follow people who have similar teaching philosophies as you, but it is just as important to find others online who challenge your thinking and help you grow as an educator and person.

One year, I posted a video of a song I taught my students to help them round numbers. It was a play on Queen's "We Will Rock You," but the words were changed to "We Will Round You." Cute, right? It *may* have been cute, but I had someone reach out to me and explain that by teaching my students how to round numbers with this song, I was taking away their ability to conceptually understand *why* we round numbers up and down. Instead, I should have used a numberline. At first, I thought, "it's a *song*, I don't understand why she is being so insistent that I'm wrong." But I was. I was wrong. After taking some time to process and reflect, I was able to understand that the way I was teaching this skill deprived my students of building their number sense. I ended up reaching out to this teacher and thanking her for pointing out the error in my ways and immediately bought a book she recommended to me about math tricks that teachers should stop using and instead teach the same skills conceptually.

Could I have ignored her feedback and continued on with my life? I could have. However, I've learned that if I'm faced with a post from someone else or feedback that makes me feel defensive, I need to lean into that feeling and process why I feel defensive. Most of the time it's because someone else directly or indirectly pointed out something that I thought was a good idea and in hindsight, wasn't. Taking and processing feedback can be hard. It's a learned skill that no one prepares you for, but it's what helps us continue to grow as lifelong learners. I purposefully follow educators who challenge my thinking and provide best practice strategies because it helps me become a better-informed teacher in my classroom.

> Taking and processing feedback can be hard. It's a learned skill that no one prepares you for, but it's what helps us continue to grow as lifelong learners.

Curating Your Feed

While working to curate your feed, ensure that your professional learning network feeds are diverse in a multitude of ways. It may sound simple, but studies show that we tend to follow people who look like us and have similar lives to our own. Therefore, it's important that we are intentionally diversifying our feeds. Check who you are following and ensure that you are following educators of different races, ethnicities, gender identities, and abilities. These accounts can help you understand education, curriculum, language, etc. from a lens that differs from your own.

You may have a specialized content area or grade level, but don't confine your feed to people who teach the exact same content. Try following a multitude of grade level teachers, content specialists, instructional coaches, administrators, and so on. High level instructional practices are cross curricular. I've used amazing ideas from college professors all the way down to kindergarten teachers. There are some ideas posted that may not work in your classroom, but they might spark an idea that you could make work in your classroom. Remember to be intentional and fill your feed with people who will help you continue to improve your craft.

How Do I Get Started?

A question I receive frequently from teachers starting new teaching accounts is, "How do I grow my following?" I'm not going to lie; I did not start my page thinking it would ever grow to what it has become. I was simply excited to share my journey with anyone who was willing to come along for the ride. However, pages and accounts that grow connections are usually the pages that post content regularly. That may sound overwhelming but think about all the things you do in the classroom in a week. A lot of times, I simply share what lessons my class completed, anchor charts I make for lessons, high leverage instructional practices such as retrieval practice, supports I integrated for differentiation, tech tools we used, and so on. You are doing so much in your classroom already and you don't have to go over the top with your content. Make it relatable so that a teacher can look at your post and think, "I could do that!" I don't go out of my way for an Instagram post, and I've found some of the things that resonated with other teachers the most were ideas I simply thought in the moment to snap a picture of.

If you're looking to curate your own page and feed my advice is simple: Share content that is helpful to others and be authentic. These two things are what I keep in mind when I share something: Is it helpful? Am I being authentic? By keeping these two things in mind, you will start to find the community you're searching for.

Finally, if you are choosing to create a page where the content is solely based on education, you *must* protect the privacy of your students. Make sure that you are not posting pictures with student faces or names in them. They have not consented to be on your page and as educators we need to not only respect that, but understand that under FERPA we are legally bound to protect the privacy of our students.

Keeping them safe is priority number one. Instead of taking pictures of your students or their work, take a picture of the exemplar you made to help guide them.

Not a Place for Comparison

Social media can be a double-edged sword. On one hand it can serve as a catalyst for extraordinary educational ideas and help you to grow your craft as an educator, but it can also make you feel like you don't measure up. Let me tell you right now: Do *not* compare yourself to others on the internet. Our lives are complex. Social media is unable to show all the small intricacies happening in someone's life. People message me regularly asking if I ever take breaks. Of course I take breaks! However, they see my Instagram feed and perceive that all I do is focus on education, lessons, grading, professional reading, and so on. Although that is indeed a very large part of my life, I *do* take time for myself. I spend a lot of time in the gym and hang out almost every minute we're not at work with my partner. I use my weekends and nights to see my family and friends. I watch *a lot* of TV, I listen to true crime podcasts and audiobooks, I enjoy cooking, and so much more. However, my page's focus is education, and I don't share those parts of my life often because it's not what my page is about. Although it may seem that I spend all my time in my classroom or doing work for my classroom, I'm doing just as much as most teachers.

It is important to know that social media is a highlight reel. For the most part, people only share the positive things happening in their lives. As a consumer of content, it's important not to compare your chapter one with someone else's chapter ten or your difficult day with someone else's "amazing" day. Know and understand that everyone's lives are just as complex and the snapshot of a lesson that they posted that day doesn't show the parent email they received that morning or the stack of papers they haven't graded. Give yourself grace and remember to take space when needed.

Social media and connecting with teachers from around the world has changed my life for the better. My professional learning network has connected me with educators from around the world who help me continue to grow as an educator. I have been lucky enough to find real friends via social media, creating an online community of support. It gave me the ability to create an international summer book club that led me to meet and collaborate with the author of *Culturize*, Jimmy Casas. Without the connection of my professional learning network, I would not be here writing this book today. I am forever grateful for the experiences, connections, and community it has afforded me. I hope you can find support and solace in an online community as well.

Be the Flame Actions

Reflect on how or if you have built a community online and consider the following:

+ How am I building rapport with other educators online?
+ Search a teaching hashtag to find ten new accounts that will rejuvenate your feed.
+ Intentionally seek out accounts that will diversify your feed.
+ Use the hashtag #BeTheFlameEDU on Instagram or Twitter and showcase how you are a *Flame in the Classroom*.

CHAPTER 8

Ablaze

Teachers must keep the flame *Ablaze* within themselves to
continue lighting flames within the people they impact.

"There is always light, if we're only brave enough to see it. If we're
only brave enough to be it."

– Amanda Gorman

Working as an educator has been one of the best experiences of my life. Not many people have the chance to make a positive impact on others whether that be a student, family member, coworker, or a person within a professional learning network each day. I am humbled by this opportunity to spread the ideas and strategies that are at the heart of my practice as an educator. Thanks to many colleagues who have modeled the way, I recognize the power of sharing and collaborating with others to continue our growth and spark new impactful ideas.

Each back-to-school season, I'm asked by a soon-to-be first year teacher what advice I have for them as they embark upon this new adventure. I always explain that the most important thing is to make time to build relationships with your students and create community within your classroom.

My most significant accomplishment in the classroom, above test scores and room set up, is cultivating strong communities with and among my students and creating an environment for each one to thrive as an individual and as a member of a team. Classroom community truly creates a space for students to feel safe and take risks in their learning. There is nothing more heartwarming than bringing a school year to a close and having students say that our class, specifically the kids in it, was one of the best classes they ever had because they felt loved and supported.

Research shows that students cannot learn when their brains are consistently in survival mode at school because they do not feel safe in their environment (Hammond, 2015). As educators, we must work to create a space for all to feel safe, feel seen, feel supported, and feel successful. That is why building individual relationships on top of fostering a community is important. Meeting individual needs of students allows them to open up and feel safe to let others, including their peers, in. This will create a strong foundation for academic growth and meeting high learning and behavioral expectations. Be mindful of keeping your flame ablaze, remembering that:

Kindling a community takes time. A community is not built overnight. Making the time to integrate team building at the beginning of the year and throughout the year to keep up the momentum is working towards an even stronger community.

Stoking a community takes persistence. Remember, as educators, we are not only teaching our standards, but the unwritten social curriculum as well. We teach reading, math, and science, but we also teach students how to be kind, understanding, and to collaborate respectfully.

Collaboration is not innate and must be taught. This will take time and patience; mistakes will be made, but those mistakes are fantastic learning opportunities for the future.

Don't be afraid if your flame flickers. Whether trying a new strategy for a lesson or troubleshooting a relationship with a student, it's never going to be perfect the first time around. However, we can only strengthen our flame if we start somewhere and make the commitment to try. Bonus: if we make a mistake, it's one more opportunity to normalize mistake making.

Know when to refuel. At times, the light dims and we become worn down—its a reality of our profession. This is a sign to take care of ourselves. There is a well-known saying that we cannot pour from an empty cup, and as flames, we cannot ignite others if we are smoldering. Find time to take care of yourself. People will care *about* you, but only you can care *for* you.

Relationships with families can look different. Part of building relationships with families is knowing their family dynamics and structures. Know that all families want their children to succeed, but not all have the ability to fit the "traditional" mold of what "parent involvement" may look like. Being understanding and supportive while keeping connected to let them know you're on their team.

Don't allow others to extinguish your flame. Do not let the judgment of others or the fear of what they may think about you change what you do in the classroom. Surround yourself with a support system of people who understand celebrating your success does not infringe on their success. Your support system should be your fuel to grow your flame, not extinguish it.

Light those around you. Think of a birthday candle: When you light one birthday candle, you can use that one candle to light the rest of the candles. Your influence can inspire greatness in others and encourage those around you to be flames in their lives as well. Continue to spread your influence and light up those around you.

Shine bright. Be bold in your endeavors. Remember that you are your own unique flame and comparing yourself to another flame is like comparing apples and oranges. Focus on your light; Shine boldly and brightly for those that you impact.

As you continue on your journey as an educator, remember the influence you have in sparking positive communities. You are the driving force of relationship building and hold the potential to ignite the power of a strong community in your classroom and in all other realms of your professional reach.

- Reflect on the educators in your past who **sparked** an impactful relationship with you.
- **Kindle** one-on-one relationships with students in order to create a safe environment for them and to show them you care for them.
- **Ignite** the community among your students, building a foundation of trust and support.
- **Stoke** that classroom community to develop it into a culture of collaboration.
- Work to **catch** on to your families, partnering with them to support their child.
- Create a community within your school that **fuels** your flame.
- **Spread** your ideas like wildfire using a professional learning network.

Above all, remember to always *Be the Flame.*

References

Agarwal, P. K. & Bain, P. M. (2019). *Powerful teaching: Unleash the science of learning.* Jossey-Bass.

Gonzalez, J. (Host). (2013-present). *Cult of Pedagogy* [Audio Podcast]. Cult of Pedagogy. https://www.cultofpedagogy.com/pod/

Hammond, Z. (2015). *Culturally responsive teaching and the brain: Promoting authentic engagement and rigor among culturally and linguistically diverse students.* Corwin.

About the Author

Shane Saeed is a fourth-grade educator in Colorado. She has been teaching fourth grade for the past seven years. Shane received her Bachelor's in psychology and an elementary teaching license from the University of Colorado at Boulder. Since then, she has earned a first Master's degree in Curriculum and Instruction with a focus in literacy and a second Master's degree in School Leadership. Currently, she is working on her doctoral degree in School Leadership with a focus on equity. Shane's passion is sharing instructional practices with educators near and far. She has presented for *Get Your Teach On* both virtually and in-person at their national conference. She facilitates professional development within her own district and serves as a guest speaker on differentiation in the classroom for Metro State University in Denver. Shane continues to teach in Colorado and collaborate with teachers across the globe via her Instagram: @fantasticallyfourth. Connect with Shane via Instagram, Twitter (@saeed_shane), or email: fantasticallyfourth@gmail.com

More from
ConnectEDD Publishing

Since 2015, ConnectEDD has worked to transform education by empowering educators to become better-equipped to teach, learn, and lead. What started as a small company designed to provide professional learning events for educators has grown to include a variety of services to help teachers and administrators address essential challenges. ConnectEDD offers instructional and leadership coaching, professional development workshops focusing on a variety of educational topics, a roster of nationally recognized educator associates who possess hands-on knowledge and experience, educational conferences custom-designed to meet the specific needs of schools, districts, and state/national organizations, and ongoing, personalized support, both virtually and onsite. In 2020, ConnectEDD expanded to include publishing services designed to provide busy educators with books and resources consisting of practical information on a wide variety of teaching, learning, and leadership topics. Please visit us online at connecteddpublishing.com or contact us at: info@connecteddpublishing.com

Recent Publications:

Live Your Excellence: Action Guide by Jimmy Casas

Culturize: Action Guide by Jimmy Casas

Daily Inspiration for Educators: Positive Thoughts for Every Day of the Year by Jimmy Casas

Eyes on Culture: Multiply Excellence in Your School by Emily Paschall

Pause. Breathe. Flourish. Living Your Best Life as an Educator by William D. Parker

L.E.A.R.N.E.R. Finding the True, Good, and Beautiful in Education by Marita Diffenbaugh

Educator Reflection Tips Volume II: Refining Our Practice by Jami Fowler-White

Handle With Care: Managing Difficult Situations in Schools with Dignity and Respect by Jimmy Casas and Joy Kelly

Disruptive Thinking: Preparing Learners for Their Future by Eric Sheninger

Permission to be Great: Increasing Engagement in Your School by Dan Butler

Made in the USA
Las Vegas, NV
10 August 2021

27896783R00092